Lesson Plans for Classroom Teachers

Third and Fourth Grades

Robert P. Pangrazi
Arizona State University

Allyn and Bacon
Boston · London · Toronto · Sydney · Tokyo · Singapore

Copyright © 1997 by Allyn & Bacon
A Viacom Company
160 Gould Street
Needham Heights, Massachusetts 02194

Internet: www.abacon.com
America Online: keyword: College Online

ISBN 0-205-19364-1

Printed in the United States of America

10 9 8 7 6 5 4 3 2   01 00 99

Library of Congress Cataloging-in-Publication Data

Pangrazi, Robert P.
   Lesson plans for classroom teachers. Third and fourth grade /
 Robert P. Pangrazi.
       p.   cm.
   ISBN 0-205-19364-1 (pbk.)
   1. Physical education for children. 2. Movement education.
3. Lesson planning. 4. Third grade (Education)--Curricula.
5. Fourth grade (Education)--Curricula.   I. Title.
 GV443.P34436 1996
 372.86043--dc21
                                                       96-46651
                                                         CIP

LESSON PLANS FOR THE SCHOOL YEAR
Third and Fourth Grade

WEEK	INTRODUCTORY ACTIVITY	FITNESS DEVELOPMENT ACTIVITY	LESSON FOCUS ACTIVITY	GAME ACTIVITY	PAGE
1	Move and Freeze on Signal	Teacher Leader Movement Challenges	Orientation	Class Management Games	1
2	Fundamental Movements and Stopping	Teacher Leader Exercises	Manipulative Skills Using Beanbags	Galloping Lizzie Crows and Cranes	3
3	Move and Assume Pose	Teacher Leader Exercises	Throwing Skills (1)	Whistle Mixer Couple Tag Partner Stoop	5
4	Walk, Trot, and Sprint	Teacher Leader Exercises	Soccer Related Activities(1)	Circle Kickball Soccer Touch Ball Diagonal Soccer Soccer Take-Away	7
5	Partner Over and Under	Teacher Leader Exercises	Soccer Related Activities (2)	Diagonal Soccer Soccer Touch Ball Dribblerama Bull's eye	9
6	Run, Stop, Pivot	Circuit Training	Fundamental Skills Through Playground Games	Playground Games	12
7	European Rhythmic Running	Circuit Training	Long Rope Jumping Skills	Trades Fly Trap Fox Hunt	13
8	Magic Number Challenges	Circuit Training	Manipulative Skills Using Playground Balls	Bounce Ball One Step	15
9	Fastest Tag in the West	Walk, Trot, and Jog	Throwing Skills (2)	In the Prison Snowball Center Target Throw Target Ball Throw	17
10	Group Tag	Walk, Trot, and Jog	Walking and Jogging Skills	Recreational Activity	19
11	Locomotor and Manipulative Activity	Walk, Trot, and Jog	Rhythmic Movement (1)	Whistle March Arches Home Base	21
12	Movement Varieties	Astronaut Drills	Hockey Related Activities (1)	Circle Keepaway Star Wars Hockey Lane Hockey Circle Straddleball	24
13	New Leader	Astronaut Drills	Hockey Related Activities (2)	Modified Hockey Lane Hockey	27
14	Group Over and Under	Astronaut Drills	Individual Rope Jumping Skills	Trades Follow Me Beachball Bat Ball	29

WEEK	INTRODUCTORY ACTIVITY	FITNESS DEVELOPMENT ACTIVITY	LESSON FOCUS ACTIVITY	GAME ACTIVITY	PAGE
15	Addition Tag	Continuity Drills	Stunts and Tumbling Skills (1)	Whistle Mixer Circle Contests Alaska Baseball	32
16	Following Activity	Continuity Drills	Rhythmic Movement (2)	Fox Hunt Steal the Treasure Addition Tag	36
17	Partner Leaping	Aerobic Fitness and Partner Resistance Exercises	Football Related Activities (1)	Football End Ball Five Passes	39
18	Bridges by Three	Aerobic Fitness and Partner Resistance Exercises	Basketball Related Activities (1)	Birdie in the Cage Dribblerama Captain Ball Basketball Tag	41
19	Jumping and Hopping Patterns	Fitness Challenges and Rope Jumping	Basketball Related Activities (2)	Captain Ball Five Passes Around the Key	44
20	Yarnball Fun	Fitness Challenges and Rope Jumping	Recreational Activities	Recreational Activities	47
21	Move and Manipulate	Fitness Challenges and Rope Jumping	Fundamental Skills Using Balance Beams	Nonda's Car Lot Fly Trap	48
22	Moving to Music	Aerobic Fitness	Stunts and Tumbling Skills (2)	Partner Stoop Crows and Cranes	50
23	European Rhythmic Running with Variations	Aerobic Fitness	Manipulative Skills Using Wands and Hoops	Home Base Indianapolis 500 Nine Lives	53
24	Tortoise and Hare	Aerobic Fitness	Rhythmic Movement (3)	Jump the Shot Beachball Batball Club Guard	56
25	Bend, Stretch, and Shake	Astronaut Drills	Volleyball Related Skills (1)	Beachball Volleyball Informal Volleyball	60
26	Move, Perform Task	Astronaut Drills	Volleyball Related Skills (2)	Beachball Volleyball Shower Service Ball	62
27	Find Your Home	Continuity Drills	Manipulative Skills Using Paddle and Balls	Steal the Treasure Trees	64
28	Combination Movement Patterns	Continuity Drills	Stunts and Tumbling Skills (3)	Trades Beachball Batball	66

Using The Lesson Plans

The lesson plans provide a guide for presenting movement experiences in a sequential and well-ordered manner. The series of plans serve as a comprehensive curriculum. Lessons can be modified and shaped to meet the needs of individual teachers. Many teachers take activities from the lesson plans and write them on 4" by 6" note cards. All lesson presentations should be mentally rehearsed to prevent excessive use of written notes. Lesson plan note cards help relieve the burden of trying to remember the proper sequence of activities and the worry of forgetting key points of instruction.

Grade Levels

Three sets of lesson plans are available to cover the Kindergarten through sixth grade curriculum. The following is a brief description about the content included in each set of lesson plans:

Kindergarten through Second Grade. Learner characteristics of children in grades K-2 dictate the need for an enjoyable and instructional learning environment. By stressing the joy of physical activity, positive behaviors are developed that last a lifetime. The majority of activities for younger children are individual in nature and center on learning movement concepts through theme development. Children learn about basic movement principles and educational movement themes are used to teach body identification and body management skills.

Third Grade through Fourth Grade. Activities for children in this age group focus on refinement of fundamental skills and the introduction of specialized sport skills. Visual-tactile coordination is enhanced by using a variety of manipulative skills. Children should be allowed the opportunity to explore, experiment, and create activities without fear. While not stressing conformity, children need to absorb the how and also the why of activity patterns. Cooperation with peers is important as more emphasis is placed on group and team activities. Initial instruction in sport skills begins at this level and a number of lead-up activities are utilized so youngsters can apply newly learned skills in a small group setting.

Fifth Grade through Sixth Grade. Physical education instruction moves toward specialized skills and sport activities. Football, basketball, softball, track and field, volleyball, and hockey are added to the sport offerings. Students continue learning and improving sport skills while participating in cooperative sport lead-up games. Less emphasis is placed on movement concept activities and a larger percentage of instructional time is devoted to manipulative activity. Adequate time is set aside for the rhythmic program and for the program area involving apparatus, stunts, and tumbling. At this level, increased emphasis is placed on physical fitness and developmental activities. Organized and structured fitness routines are offered so that students can begin to make decisions about personal approaches to maintaining fitness levels.

Format of the Lesson Plans

Each lesson plan is divided into four instructional parts and contains enough activities for a week of instruction. Briefly, the four instructional parts of the lesson plan and major purposes of each section are as follows:

Introductory Activity: Introductory activities change weekly and are used to physiologically prepare children for activity when entering the gymnasium or activity area. Activities used in this section demand little instruction and allow time for practicing class management skills.

Fitness Development Activity: Fitness activities take 7 to 8 minutes of a 30 minute lesson. The activities should be personalized, progressive in nature, and exercise all parts of the body. Allied to the workout should be brief discussions about the values of fitness for a healthy lifestyle. A comprehensive discussion of fitness principles, fitness activities, and instructional guidelines is found in Chapter 8 of the textbook.

Lesson Focus Activities: The purpose of the lesson focus is to teach children major program objectives such as the development of eye-hand coordination, body management competency, and fundamental and specialized skills (e.g., folk dancing, shooting a basket, and catching an object). The lesson focus uses 15-20 minutes of the daily lesson depending on the length of the teaching period. Lesson focus activities are organized into units and vary in length depending on the developmental level of children. Lesson focus activities are changed weekly except when continuity of instruction demands longer units. Enough activities are placed in each lesson focus section to accommodate three to four teaching periods.

The content in each lesson is organized in a developmental sequence, with the first activity being the easiest and the last activity the most difficult. Usually, instruction starts with the first activity and proceeds forward regardless of developmental level. The implications are twofold: This progression ensures that each unit begins with success, since all children are capable of performing the beginning activities. It also assures that a proper sequence of activities will be followed during instruction. Obviously, developmentally mature children will progress further along the continuum of activities than less capable children.

Game Activity: This part of the lesson plan takes place at the closing of the lesson, utilizing the last 5-7 minutes of the period. Games are often used as a culminating activity for practicing skills emphasized in the lesson focus. In other lessons, games are unrelated to the lesson focus and are presented for the purpose of completing the lesson with a fun and enjoyable activity. The game should leave children with positive feelings so they look forward with anticipation to the next lesson. If the lesson has been physically demanding, a less active game can be played and vice versa. In some cases, a low key, relaxing activity might be chosen so that children can unwind before returning to the classroom.

Contents of the Lesson Plans

Objectives and required equipment are listed at the top of each lesson plan. This establishes the reason for teaching the lesson and makes it easy to prepare the equipment for instruction. The contents of the lesson plans is placed into two columns:

Instructional Activities: This column lists activities that will be taught in the lesson. The content in this column offers progression and sequence for activities that will be presented during the week. All activities are explained in detail and can be presented easily from each lesson plan.

Teaching Hints: This section provides points for efficient organization of the class and important learning cues. Emphasis in this column is on teaching for quality of movement rather than quantity.

Lesson Plans for Grades 3-4 - Week 1
Orientation and Class Management Activities

Objectives:
To learn and follow basic management activities necessary for participation in
   physical education classes

Equipment Required:
Tom-tom
Tape player and music for fitness
   challenges

Instructional Activities	Teaching Hints

Orientation Instructional Procedures

The first week of school should be used to teach students the system you are going to use throughout the year. The following are reminders you might find useful in establishing your expectations and routines.

1. Establish rules and expectations. Discuss your expectations with the class to assure students understand reasons for your guidelines. Explain what the consequences are when rules are not followed. Show where time-out boxes are located and how they will be used.

2. Explain to the class the method you will use to learn names. It might be helpful to ask classroom teachers to have students put their name on a piece of masking tape (name tag). Tell students that you will ask them their name on a regular basis until it is learned.

3. Develop entry and exit behaviors for students coming and leaving physical education classes. Students should know how to enter the instructional area and to leave equipment alone until told to use it. If squads are used for instruction, place students into squads and practice moving into formation on signal.

4. Decide how excuses for non-participation will be handled. If possible, set up a routine where the school nurse determines which students are excused for health reasons.

5. Safety is important. Children should receive safety rules to be followed on apparatus and playground equipment. Safety procedures to be followed in physical education classes should be discussed.

6. Illustrate how you will stop and start the class. In general, a whistle (or similar loud signal) and a raised hand is effective for stopping the class. A voice command should be used to start the class. Telling the class when before what (Chapter ??) will assure they do not begin before instructions are finished.

7. Discuss the issue, distribution, and care of equipment. Make students responsible for acquiring a piece of equipment and returning it at the end of the lesson. Place equipment around the perimeter of the teaching area to reduce the chance of students fighting over a piece of equipment.

8. Explain to the class that the format of the daily lesson will include an introductory activity, fitness development, lesson focus, and finish with a game activity.

9. Practice various teaching formations such as open-squad formation and closed-squad formation. Practice moving into a circle while moving (fall-in). Transitions between formations should be done while moving, i.e., jogging from scatter formation into a circular formation.

10. Refer to Chapters 4 and 5 in the text for detailed information about planning, developing an effective learning environment, and class management strategies.

Introductory Activity -- Move and Freeze on Signal

Have students move throughout the area using a variety of locomotor movements. On signal (whistle), they quickly freeze. Try to reduce the response latency by reinforcing students who stop quickly on signal.

The primary objective is to teach students the importance of moving under control (without bumping others or falling down) and quickly freezing.

Fitness Development Activity -- Teacher Leader Movement Challenges

1. Locomotor Movement: Walk for 30 seconds.

2. Flexibility and Trunk Development Challenges
   a. Bend in different directions.
   b. Stretch slowly and return quickly.
   c. Combine bending and stretching movements.
   d. Sway back and forth.
   e. Twist one body part; add body parts.

3. Locomotor Movement: Skip for 30 seconds.

4. Shoulder Girdle Challenges
   In a push-up position, do the following challenges:
   a. Lift one foot; the other foot.
   b. Wave at a friend; wave with the other arm.
   c. Scratch your back with one hand; use the other hand.
   d. Walk your feet to your hands.

5. Locomotor Movement: Jog for 30 seconds.

6. Abdominal Development Challenges
   From a supine position:
   1. Lift your head and look at your toes.
   2. Lift your knees to your chest.
   3. Wave your legs at a friend.
   From a sitting position;
   1. Slowly lay down with hands on tummy.
   2. Lift legs and touch toes.

7. Locomotor Movement: Run and leap for 30 seconds.

The goal should be to move students through a number of movement challenges. Emphasis should be placed on starting the fitness activities at a level where all students can feel successful.

See text, p. 163-167 for descriptions of challenges.

Alternate the locomotor movements with the strength and flexibility challenges. Repeat the challenges as necessary.

Tape alternating segments (30 seconds in length) of silence and music to signal duration of exercise. Music segments indicate locomotor movements while intervals of silence announce doing the movement challenges.

Teach youngsters the different challenges and then allow them to select a challenge they can successfully perform.

Encourage students to focus on effort and feeling successful.

Workloads should be moderate with emphasis on success for all youngsters.

Lesson Focus – Orientation

Since much time during the first week is used for orientation procedures and management, no lesson focus activity is scheduled.

Game Activity -- Management Games

Play one or two management games to teach students how to move into partner and small group formation

Back to Back
   Supplies: None
   Skills: Fundamental locomotor movements
   Students move under control throughout the area using a variety of locomotor movements. On signal, each child stands back to back (or toe to toe) with another child. If one child ends up without a partner, the teacher takes this student as a partner. Youngsters who do not find a partner nearby run to a designated spot in the center of the area. This helps assure that students do not run around looking for a partner or feel left out. Students who move to the center spot quickly find a partner and move out of the area (to avoid crowding around the center spot). Emphasis should be placed finding a partner near them, not searching for a friend, and taking a different partner each time.

Whistle Mixer
   Supplies: None
   Skills: All basic locomotor movements
   Children are scattered throughout the area. To begin, they move in any direction they wish. The teacher whistles a number of times in succession and raises the same number of fingers above their head to signal the group size. Children then form small groups with the number in each group equal to the number of whistles. For example, if there are four short whistles, children form circles of four--no more, no less. The goal is to find the correct number of students as quickly as possible. As soon as a group has the desired number, they sit down to signal that other may not join the group. Children who cannot find a group nearby should move to the center of the area and raise their hands to facilitate finding others without a group.

Lesson Plans for Grades 3-4 - Week 2
Manipulative Skills Using Beanbags

Objectives:
To stop quickly and under control
To maintain the fitness development activity
To toss and catch an object in a variety of situations

Equipment Required:
One beanbag for each student
Music tape for exercises

Instructional Activities	Teaching Hints

Introductory Activity -- Fundamental Movements and Stopping

Use the locomotor movements (run, walk, hop, jump, leap, slide, gallop and skip) to move throughout the instructional area. On signal, students stop and freeze without falling. Teach proper stopping form, lowering the center of gravity, spreading the feet for a wide base of support, and keeping the body weight over the feet (minimize leaning). This is an excellent activity for teaching students to move in their own space (as far away from others as possible).

Tape alternating segments of silence and music to signal duration of the locomotor movements. Segments of silence that indicate the "freeze" position can be decreased in duration until the desired response latency is reached.

Fitness Development Activity -- Teacher Leader Exercises

Arm Circles	25 seconds
Bend and Twist	25 seconds
Treadmill	25 seconds
Abdominal Challenges	25 seconds
Single-Leg Crab Kick	25 seconds
Knee to Chest Curl	25 seconds
Run in Place	25 seconds
Trunk Twister	25 seconds

Conclude the routine with 2 to 4 minutes of jogging, rope jumping or other continuous activity.

Tape alternating segments of silence (10 seconds) to signal a change of exercise and music to signal the duration of exercise (25 seconds).

Allow students to adjust the workload to their personal ability and fitness level. This means that some students will perform more repetitions than others.

See text, p. 174-186 for descriptions of exercises.

Lesson Focus -- Beanbag Activities

In place, Tossing to self
1. Toss and catch with both hands - right hand, left hand
2. Toss and catch with the back of hands. This will encourage children to catch with "soft hands."
3. Toss the beanbag to increasingly high level, *emphasizing* a straight overhead toss. To encourage straight tossing, have the child sit down.

Give students two or three activities to practice so you have time to move and help youngsters. Alternate activities from each of the categories so students receive a variety of skills to practice.

In Place, Adding Stunts
1. Toss overhead and perform the following stunts and catch the bag.
   a. 1/4 and 1/2 turns, right and left
   b. Full turn
   c. Touch floor
   d. Clap hands
   e. Clap hands around different parts of body, behind back, under legs.
   f. Heel click
   g. Student choice

Stress a soft receipt of the beanbag by giving with the hands, arms, and legs. "Giving" involves the hands going out toward the incoming beanbag and bringing it in for a soft landing.

Remind students to keep their eyes on the beanbag when catching.

In place, kicking to self
1. Place beanbag on foot, kick up and catch--right foot, left foot.
2. Try above activity from sitting and lying positions.
3. Kick up and catch behind back.
4. Kick up overhead, make ½ turn and catch.
5. Put beanbag between feet, jump up and catch beanbag.
6. Toss beanbag with one foot and catch with the other foot.

When tossing and catching, toss slightly above eye level. Overly high tosses should be discouraged until catching is mastered.

Locomotor movements (Toss, Move and Catch)
1. Toss overhead, move to another spot and catch.
2. Toss, do a locomotor movement and catch.
3. Move from side to side.
4. Toss overhead behind self, move and catch.
5. Exploratory movements.

Balance the beanbag
1. Balance on the following body parts:
    a. Head
    b. Back of hand
    c. Shoulder
    d. Knee
    e. Foot
    f. Elbow
2. Balance and move as follows:
    a. Walk
    b. Run
    c. Skip
    d. Gallop
    e. Sit down
    f. Lie down
    g. Turn around
    h. Balance beanbag on body part and move on all fours.

Partner activities
1. Toss back and forth using the following throws:
    a. Two-handed throws--overhead, underhand, side and over shoulder.
    b. One-handed throws and catches.
    c. Throw at different levels and targets such as high, low, left, right.
    d. Throw under leg, around body, from behind back, center, as in football, etc.
    e. Sit down and play catch--try different throws and catches.
    f. Toss in various directions to make partner move and catch. Have one partner move around other in a circle while catching and throwing.
    g. Propel more than one beanbag back and forth. Toss both beanbags together, as well as at opposite times.

Beanbags should be at least 6 inches square. This size balances well and can be controlled on various parts of the body, thus offering greater challenge.

Stress laterality and directionality when teaching manipulative skills. Children should be taught to throw, catch, and balance beanbags with both the left and right sides of their body. They should learn to catch and throw at different levels.

See who can balance the beanbag longest on various body parts while moving.

Emphasize quality not quantity. Motivation is often enhanced by practicing an activity for a short time and returning to it later.

Children should toss at chest height to a partner, unless a different type of throw is specified. Teach all types of return: low, medium, high, left, and right.

In partner work, keep distances between partners reasonable, especially in introductory phases. Fifteen feet or so seems to be a reasonable starting distance. Throwing too hard or out of range, to cause the partner to miss, should be discussed.

Game Activity

Galloping Lizzie
> Supplies: A beanbag or fleece ball
> Skills: Throwing, dodging, running

One player is it and has a beanbag or fleece ball. The other players are scattered around the playground. The player with the bag or ball runs after the others and attempts to hit another player below the shoulders with the object. The person hit becomes it, and the game continues. The tagger must throw the bag or ball, not merely touch another person with it.
Variation: A pair of children is it, with one of the players handling the bag or ball. A specific kind of toss can be called for (e.g., overhand, underhand, left-handed).

Crows and Cranes
> Supplies: None
> Skills: Running, dodging

Two goal lines are drawn about 50 ft apart. Children are divided into two groups—the crows and the cranes. The groups face each other at the center of the area, about 5 ft apart. The leader calls out either "Crows" or "Cranes," using a cr-r-r-r-r sound at the start of either word to mask the result. If "Crows" is the call, the crows chase the cranes to the goal line. If "Cranes" is the call, then the cranes chase. Any child caught goes over to the other side. The team that has the most players when the game ends is the winner.

Lesson Plans for Grades 3-4 - Week 3
Throwing Skills (1)

Objectives:
To recognize a variety of shapes and move the body into the correct shape
To perform continuous fitness activity
To know the elements of proper throwing
To throw with maximum velocity

Equipment Required:
Many types of balls for throwing
Throwing targets; hoops, mats, bowling
    pins and/or cageball
Tape for exercises
Whistle

Instructional Activities	Teaching Hints

Introductory Activity -- Move and Assume Shape

Have students move using a variation of a basic movement. Freeze on signal and assume a designated shape. Some suggestions are:
    a. Balance
    b. Stretch
    c. Curl
    d. Bridge

Encourage creativity in movements and poses.

Reinforce moving under control.

Use scatter formation.

Fitness Development Activity -- Teacher Leader Exercises

Arm Circles	30 seconds
Sitting Stretch	30 seconds
Treadmill	30 seconds
Abdominal Challenges	30 seconds
Single-Leg Crab Kick	30 seconds
Knee to Chest Curl	30 seconds
Power Jumper	30 seconds
Trunk Twister	30 seconds

Conclude the routine with 2 to 4 minutes of jogging, rope jumping or other continuous activity.

Tape alternating segments of silence (10 seconds) to signal a change of exercise and music to signal the duration of exercise (30 seconds).

Increase the duration of exercises by 10 to 20% over the previous week.

See text, p. 174-186 for descriptions of exercises.

Lesson Focus -- Throwing Skills

Individual activities
1. Throw balls against the wall. Emphasize the following points:
    a. Start with the feet together.
    b. Start with non-throwing side to the wall.
    c. Lift both the throwing and non-throwing arm (to form a "T" in order to assure the throwing arm elbow is lifted and the non-throwing arm points at the target.
    d. Begin the throw with a step forward with the foot opposite the throwing arm.
    e. Throw as hard as possible.
2. Throw from one side of the gym and try to hit the other wall.
3. If outside, throw as hard and far as possible.

Throwing for form
1. Arrange activities to emphasize proper throwing form. Some suggestions are:
    a. Throwing off a tumbling mat. The slight step down off the mat helps some students develop the forward step with the non-throwing side foot. The student stands on the edge of the mat and steps to the floor with the non-throwing side foot as the throw begins. (The other foot remains on the mat). Use the cues, "step, elbow leads, and throw.
    b. Starting a throw with both feet in a hoop. The thrower must lift the front foot to step out of the hoop. Begin with the non-throwing side of the body facing the target and both feet inside the hoop. As the throw begins, a forward step is taken with the non-throwing foot out of the hoop.

Throwing takes a great deal of practice to master. Two major issues to consider when teaching throwing are:
1. How can I arrange my class so students receive the most opportunity to throw?
2. How can I arrange my class so students get to throw with maximum velocity. A mature pattern of throwing cannot be learned if students are not allowed to throw with maximum force.

Proper form and velocity of throws are closely related. A reason for practicing form is to encourage students to think about technique.

Give each student 4 or 5 balls to throw. They can be placed in a frisbee to keep them from rolling around. When all the balls have been thrown by all the students, students go retrieve the same number of balls they have thrown.

c. Touching a cone behind the thrower. The thrower lines up with a cone about an arms-length away and near the throwing side (away from the target). As the throwing arm is extended on the backswing, a slight backward reach is made to encourage reaching back in preparation to throw.

Throwing for velocity

1. Throw at mats on the wall
   a. Throw fleece balls hard from 15 to 20 feet
   b. Retrieve only if the balls roll behind the throwing line.
2. Throw at hoops leaning against the wall and try to knock them down.
3. Throw at bowling pins
4. Throw outside for distance.

Throwing for velocity is exciting for youngsters. It can also increase the activity level of the lesson as youngsters retrieve the thrown objects.

A cageball is an excellent target for encouraging throwing velocity. When it is hit, it will move slightly. A goal can be made to move the cageball across a goal line.

Game Activity

Whistle Mixer

Supplies: A whistle

Skills: All basic locomotor movements

Children are scattered throughout the area. To begin, they walk around in any direction they wish. The teacher blows a whistle a number of times in succession with short, sharp blasts. Children then form small circles with the number in the circles equal to the number of whistle blasts. If there are four blasts, children form circles of four--no more, no less. The goal is not to be left out or caught in a circle with the incorrect number of students. Children should be encouraged to move to the center of the area and raise their hands to facilitate finding others without a group.

After the circles are formed, the teacher calls "Walk," and the game continues. In walking, children should move in different directions.

Variation: A fine version of this game is done with the aid of a tom-tom. Different beats indicate different locomotor movements--skipping, galloping, slow walking, normal walking, running. The whistle is still used to set the number for each circle.

Couple Tag

Supplies: None

Skills: Running, dodging

Two goal lines are established about 50 ft apart. Children run in pairs, with inside hands joined. All pairs, except one, line up on one of the goal lines. The pair in the center is it. They call "Come on over," and the children, keeping hands joined, run to the other goal line. The pair in the center, also retaining joined hands, tries to tag any other pair. As soon as a couple is caught, they help the center couple. The game continues until all are caught. The last couple caught is it for the next game.

Variation: <u>Triplet Tag</u>. The game can be played with sets of threes. Tagging is done with any pair of joined hands. If a triplet breaks joined hands, it is considered caught.

Partner Stoop

Supplies: Music

Skills: Marching rhythmically

The game follows the same basic principle of stooping as in Circle Stoop, but it is played with partners. The group forms a double circle, with partners facing counterclockwise, which means that one partner is on the inside and one is on the outside. When the music begins, all march in the line of direction. After a short period of marching, a signal (whistle) is sounded, and the inside circle reverses direction and marches the other way--clockwise. The partners are thus separated. When the music stops, the outer circle stands still, and the partners making up the inner circle walk to rejoin their respective outer circle partners. As soon as a child reaches her partner, they join inside hands and stoop without losing balance. The last couple to stoop and those who have lost balance go to the center of the circle and wait out the next round.

Insist that players walk when joining their partner. This avoids the problem of stampeding and colliding with others.

Lesson Plans for Grades 3-4 - Week 4
Soccer Related Activities (1)

Objectives:
To strike a foam rubber soccer ball with a variety of body parts
To dribble a foam rubber soccer ball with the feet
To trap a foam rubber ball with a variety of body parts
To play a soccer lead-up activity and understand the joy of participation

Equipment Required:
8" foam rubber or 8½" playground ball
  for each student
Music tape for exercises
Pinnies (optional)
Cones for marking the drill areas and
  goals

Instructional Activities	Teaching Hints

Introductory Activity -- Walk, Trot and Sprint

Youngsters move throughout the area and change the pace of their movement depending on the number of signals (whistles or tom-tom beats) given. When four signals are given, the class freezes and performs a variety of stretches.
1. One signal—walk
2. Two signals—trot
3. Three signals—run
4. Whistle--freeze and stretch

Emphasize moving under control. Students should never run as fast as possible, but rather at a speed where they can stop quickly.

Reinforce students who respond quickly to the signal.

Fitness Development Activity -- Teacher Leader Exercises

Arm Circles	35 seconds
Bend and Twist	35 seconds
Treadmill	35 seconds
Abdominal Challenges	35 seconds
Single-Leg Crab Kick	35 seconds
Knee to Chest Curl	35 seconds
Run in Place	35 seconds
Standing Hip Bend	35 seconds

Conclude the routine with 2 to 4 minutes of jogging, rope jumping or other
  continuous activity.

Tape alternating segments of silence (10 seconds) to signal a change of exercise and music to signal the duration of exercise (35 seconds).

Allow students to adjust the workload to their ability and fitness level. This means that some students will perform more repetitions than others.

See text, p. 174-186 for descriptions of exercises.

Lesson Focus -- Soccer Related Activities (1)

Skills
Practice the following skills:
1. Dribbling
   Dribbling is moving the ball with a series of taps or pushes to cover ground and still retain control. It allows a player to change direction quickly and to avoid opponents. The best contact point is the inside of the foot, but the outside of the foot will be used at faster running speeds. The ball should be kept close to the player to maintain control.
2. Inside-of-the-Foot Pass (Push Pass)
   The inside-of-the-foot pass is used for accurate passing over distances of up to 15 yards. Because of the technique used, this pass is sometimes referred to as the push pass. The non-kicking foot is placed well up, alongside the ball. As the kicking foot is drawn back, the toe is turned out. During the kick, the toe remains turned out so that the inside of the foot is perpendicular to the line of flight. The sole is kept parallel to the ground. At contact, the knee of the kicking leg should be well forward, over the ball, and both knees should be slightly bent.
3. Inside-of-the-Foot Trap
   This is the most common method of control, and is used when the ball is either rolling along the ground or bouncing up to knee height. The full surface of the foot, from heel to toe, should be presented perpendicular to the ball.

When teaching students beginning skills, have them place their hands behind their back to avoid the temptation of touching the ball with the hands.

Keep the ball near the body so it can be controlled. (Don't kick it too far in front of the body.) Dribble the ball with a controlled tap.

Place the non-kicking foot alongside the ball. Keep the head down and eyes focused on the ball during contact.

Make contact with the outside or inside of the foot rather than with the toe.

Move in line with the path of the ball and reach with the foot to meet the ball. Give when ball contact is made to absorb force.

Drills

Use the following partner drills to practice the skills above:

1. Dribbling, marking, and ball recovery. Pairs are scattered, with one player in each pair having a soccer ball. That player dribbles in various directions, and the second player attempts to stay close to the first (marking). As skill development occurs, the defensive player can attempt to recover the ball from the dribbler. If successful, roles are reversed.

2. Dribbling, Passing, and Trapping. One player of the pair has a ball and dribbles in different directions. On signal, she passes to her partner, who traps the ball and begins dribbling, continuing until another signal is given.

Each student should practice dribbling and handling the ball individually. Use drills after students have had time to practice the skills individually. Working with a partner increases the motivational level.

Emphasize controlled activity. The goal is not to see how far or hard the ball can be kicked.

Play the soccer lead-up games after sufficient time has been allotted for skills and drills.

Game Activity -- Soccer Lead-Up Games

Circle Kickball

Supplies: Two soccer balls or 8-in. foam rubber balls

Skills: Kicking, controlling

Players are in circle formation. Using the side of the foot, players kick the balls back and forth inside the circle. The object is to kick a ball out of the circle beneath the shoulder level of the circle players. A point is scored against each of the players where a ball leaves the circle between them. If, however, a lost ball is clearly the fault of a single player, then the point is scored against that player only. Any player who kicks a ball higher than the shoulders of the circle players has a point scored against him. Players with the fewest points scored against them win. Players must watch carefully since two balls are in action at one time. A player cannot be penalized if she leaves the circle to recover a ball and the second ball goes through her vacated spot.

Soccer Touch Ball

Supplies: A soccer ball

Skills: Kicking, controlling

Players are spaced around a circle 10 yd in diameter with two players in the center. The object of the game is to keep the players in the center from touching the ball. The ball is passed back and forth as in soccer. If a center player touches the ball with a foot, the person who kicked the ball goes to the center. If a circle player commits an error (i.e., misses a ball), the person responsible changes places with a center player. A rule that no player may contain or hold the ball longer than 3 seconds tends to keep the game moving.

Diagonal Soccer

Supplies: A soccer ball, pinnies (optional)

Skills: Kicking, passing, dribbling, some controlling, defending, blocking shots

Two corners are marked off with cones 5 ft from the corners on both the sides, outlining triangular dead areas. Each team lines up and protects two adjacent sides of the square. The dead area on the opposite corner marks the opposing team's goal lines. To begin competition, three players from each team move into the playing area in their own half of the space. These are the active players. During play, they may roam anywhere in the square. The other players act as line guards.

The object of the game is for active players to kick the ball through the opposing team's line (beneath shoulder height) to score. When a score is made, active players rotate to the sidelines and new players take their place. Players on the sidelines may block the ball with their bodies but cannot use their hands. The team against whom the point was scored starts the ball for the next point. Only active players may score. Scoring is much the same as in Circle Kickball in that a point is awarded for the opponents when any of the following occur.

1. A team allows the ball to go through its line below the shoulders.
2. A team touches the ball illegally.
3. A team kicks the ball over the other team above shoulder height.

Soccer Take-Away

Supplies: A soccer ball for each student

Skills: Dribbling and defensive skills

Four or five players are designated as defensive players. Each of the rest of the students have a soccer ball and dribble it around the area. The defensive players try to take away a ball from the offensive players. When a successful steal is made, the player losing control of the ball becomes a defensive player.

Lesson Plans for Grades 3-4 - Week 5
Soccer Related Activities (2)

Objectives:
To strike a foam rubber soccer ball with a variety of body parts
To dribble a foam rubber soccer ball with the feet
To trap a foam rubber ball with a variety of body parts
To play a soccer lead-up activity and understand the joy of participation

Equipment Required:
One 8" foam rubber or 8½" playground
ball for each student
Music tape for exercises
Pinnies for games (optional)
Cones for marking the drill areas and
goals

Instructional Activities	Teaching Hints

Introductory Activity -- Partner Over and Under

Students pair up with one person on the floor and the other standing ready to move. On signal, the standing students move over, under and/or around the persons on the floor. On signal, reverse positions.

Avoid touching partners when moving.

Students on the floor can also alternate between positions such as curl, stretch and bridge.

Fitness Development Activity -- Teacher Leader Exercises

Sitting Stretch	40 seconds
Power Jumper	40 seconds
Jumping Jacks	40 seconds
Abdominal Challenges	40 seconds
Single-Leg Crab Kick	40 seconds
Knee to Chest Curl	40 seconds
Windmill	40 seconds
Trunk twister	40 seconds

Conclude the routine with 2 to 4 minutes of jogging, rope jumping or other continuous activity.

Tape alternating segments of silence (10 seconds) to signal a change of exercise and music to signal the duration of exercise (40 seconds).

Allow students to adjust the workload to their ability and fitness level. This means that some students will perform more repetitions than others.

See text, p. 174-186 for descriptions of exercises.

Lesson Focus -- Soccer-Skills and Drills (2)

Skills

Divide the skills into four stations and place necessary equipment at each station. Students can practice skills they learned in last week's lesson.
1. Review and practice the long pass. Set up a station with plenty of room and students with a partner. They long pass back and forth to each other.
2. Review the inside-of-the foot pass and trapping: Work with a partner and practice passing and trapping.
3. Practice dribbling skills: Give each student a ball and have them practice dribbling. Move the ball with a series of taps. Start slowly and keep the ball in front of the body.
4. Dribbling and Passing: Students work with a partner. One dribbles the ball a short distance and then pass it to their partner.

Drills Using Three Players

With one ball for three players, many of the possibilities suggested for pair practice are still possible. An advantage of drills for three players is that fewer balls are needed.
1. Passing and controlling. The trio of players set up a triangle with players about 10 yards apart. Controlled passing and practice in ball control should occur.
2. Dribbling and passing. A shuttle-type drill can be structured where players keep going back and forth continuously. Player 1 has the ball and dribbles to player 2, who dribbles the ball back to player 3, who in turn dribbles to player 1. Players can dribble the entire distance or dribble a portion of the distance and then pass the ball to the end player. Obstacles can be set up to challenge players to dribble through or around each obstacle.

Make signs that tell students the skills they are to practice at each station. Set the signs on cones in the areas where students are to practice.

The foam training balls are best for teaching introductory soccer skills. They don't hurt students when kicked or when they are struck by a ball.

Grids with areas that are approximately 10 yards square can be marked off with marking spots or cones. The drills are then conducted with a threesome in each area.

The drills can also be set up as individual stations where students rotate after a specified time.

3. Dribbling and stopping the ball. Three dribblers are in line, each with a ball. The leader moves in various directions, followed by the other two players. On signal, each player controls her ball. The leader circles around to the back ball, and the other two move one ball forward. The dribbling continues for another stop. A third stop puts the players back in their original positions.
4. Passing. Players stand in three corners of a 10-yard square. After a player passes, he must move to the empty corner of the square, which is sometimes a diagonal movement.
5. Passing and defense. One player is the feeder and rolls the ball to either player. As soon as she rolls the ball, she attempts to block or tackle the player receiving the ball to prevent a pass to the third player, who, if the pass is completed, attempts to pass back.

Many of the drills are simple game activities. Students enjoy the opportunity to play with friends.

Emphasis should be on form and practicing the skills. If students are unable to control the ball, drills may not work and students should be given time to practice individually.

Game Activity -- Soccer Lead-Up Activities

Diagonal Soccer
Supplies: A soccer ball, pinnies (optional)
Skills: Kicking, passing, dribbling, some controlling, defending, blocking shots
Two corners are marked off with cones 5 ft from the corners on both the sides, outlining triangular dead areas. Each team lines up and protects two adjacent sides of the square. The dead area on the opposite corner marks the opposing team's goal lines. To begin competition, three players from each team move into the playing area in their own half of the space. These are the active players. During play, they may roam anywhere in the square. The other players act as line guards.
The object of the game is for active players to kick the ball through the opposing team's line (beneath shoulder height) to score. When a score is made, active players rotate to the sidelines and new players take their place. Players on the sidelines may block the ball with their bodies but cannot use their hands. The team against whom the point was scored starts the ball for the next point. Only active players may score. Scoring is much the same as in Circle Kickball in that a point is awarded for the opponents when any of the following occur.
1. A team allows the ball to go through its line below the shoulders.
2. A team touches the ball illegally.
3. A team kicks the ball over the other team above shoulder height.
Variations:
1. If the class is large, a bigger area and more active players can be used.
2. If scoring seems too easy, the line defenders can use their hands to stop the ball.

Soccer Touch Ball
Supplies: A soccer ball
Skills: Kicking, controlling
Players are spaced around a circle 10 yd in diameter with two players in the center. The object of the game is to keep the players in the center from touching the ball. The ball is passed back and forth as in soccer. If a center player touches the ball with a foot, the person who kicked the ball goes to the center. If a circle player commits an error (i.e., misses a ball), the person responsible changes places with a center player. A rule that no player may contain or hold the ball longer than 3 seconds tends to keep the game moving.

Dribblerama
Supplies: One soccer ball for each player
Skills: Dribbling, protecting the ball
The playing area is a large circle or square, clearly outlined. All players dribble within the area. The game is played on two levels.
Level 1: Each player dribbles throughout the area, controlling the ball so that it does not touch another ball. If a touch occurs, both players go outside the area and dribble counterclockwise around the area. Once youngsters have completed dribbling one lap of the counterclockwise path, they may reenter the game.
Level 2: While dribbling and controlling the ball, each player attempts to kick any other ball out of the area. When a ball is kicked out, the player owning that ball takes it outside and dribbles around the area. Play continues until only two or three players who have not lost control of their ball are left. These are declared the winners. Bring all players back into the game and repeat.

Bull's Eye

Supplies: One soccer ball per player

Skills: Dribbling, protecting the ball

The playing area is a large outlined area--circle, square, or rectangle. One player holds a ball in her hands, which serves as the bull's-eye. The other players dribble within the area. The player with the bull's-eye attempts to throw her ball (basketball push shot) at any other ball. The ball that is hit now becomes the new bull's-eye. The old bull's-eye becomes one of the dribblers. A new bull's-eye cannot hit back immediately at the old bull's-eye. A dribbler should protect the ball with her body. If the group is large, have two bull's-eyes. No score is kept and no one is eliminated.

Lesson Plans for Grades 3-4 - Week 6
Fundamental Skills Through Playground Games

Objectives:
To learn the rules of games that are common on local playgrounds
To learn the etiquette of games that are common on local playgrounds
To understand the recreational and self-directed nature of playground games

Equipment Required:
Signs and music for circuit training
5-6 hoops
Equipment needed for playground games

Instructional Activities	Teaching Hints

Introductory Activity -- Run, Stop and Pivot

The class should run, stop on signal and pivot. Vary the activity by having the class pivot on the left or right foot and increase the circumference of the pivot. Movement should be continuous. Students pivot and then continue running.

Relate the pivot to a sport such as basketball and explain how it involves rotating around one foot.

Fitness Development Activity -- Circuit Training

Students do the best they can at each station within the time limit. This implies that not all youngsters are required to do the same workload. Children differ and their ability to perform fitness workloads differs. Make fitness a personal challenge.
Rope Jumping
Triceps Push-Ups
Agility Run
Body Circles
Hula Hoop
Knee Touch Curl-Ups
Crab Walk
Tortoise and Hare
Bend and Twist

Conclude circuit training with 2-4 minutes of walking, jogging, rope jumping or other aerobic activity. See text, p. 191-194 for descriptions of circuit training.

Tape alternating segments of silence and music to signal duration of exercise. Music segments (begin at 30 seconds) indicate activity at each station while intervals of silence (10 seconds) announce it is time to stop and move forward to the next station.

Use signals such as start, stop, and move up to ensure rapid movement to the next station.

Ask students to do the best they can. Expect workloads to differ.

Lesson Focus and Game Activity

Fundamental Skills Through Playground Games

The objective of this lesson should be to teach youngsters the rules and methods for playing games during their free time. Emphasis should be on self-direction so students do not need supervision.
1. Tetherball
2. Four Square
3. Two Square
4. Volley Tennis
5. Basketball
   a. Around the Key
   b. Twenty One
   c. Freeze Out
6. Hopscotch
7. Jump Rope
8. Soccer (2 on 2)
9. Frisbee Golf
10. Wall Handball
11. Any recreational games played at your school.

The focus of this lesson is to teach students the rules and etiquette required to play recreational activities. Take time to discuss questions students might have about the activities.

These playground games listed here are just examples. Most schools have a number of games that are popular and played by the majority of youngsters. Ask youngsters what games are popular and allow some selected upper grade students to teach them.

If desired, set up stations and divide students into four groups. All students to rotate to each group during the lesson focus time. Use signs on cones that explain the activities to be done at each station.

Lesson Plans for Grades 3-4 - Week 7
Long-Rope Jumping Skills

Objectives:
To move rhythmically to a drumbeat
To jump a rope turned by others
To know the difference in long-rope jumping between entering front and back doors

Equipment Required:
Long-jump ropes (two for each group of
   four children)
Circuit training signs and tape
5-6 hoops
5-6 individual jump ropes

Instructional Activities	Teaching Hints

Introductory Activity -- European Rhythmic Running

To introduce a group of children to Rhythmic Running, have them clap to the beat of the drum. Next, as they clap, have them walk in place, keeping time. Following this, have them run in place, omitting the clapping. Finally, the class can run in single-file formation, develop the ability to follow a leader, maintain proper spacing and move to the rhythm of the tom-tom.

A variation is to have a leader move in different shapes and designs. Have class freeze and see if they can identify the shape or formation.

Fitness Development Activity – Circuit Training

Rope Jumping
Triceps Push-Ups
Agility Run
Body Circles
Hula Hoop
Knee Touch Curl-Ups
Crab Walk
Tortoise and Hare
Bend and Twist

Conclude circuit training with 2-4 minutes of walking, jogging, rope jumping or other aerobic activity. See text, p. 191-194 for descriptions of circuit training.

Tape alternating segments of silence and music to signal duration of exercise. Music segments (begin at 30 seconds) indicate activity at each station while intervals of silence (10 seconds) announce it is time to stop and move forward to the next station.

Use signals such as start, stop, and move up to ensure rapid movement to the next station.

See text, p. 174-186 for descriptions of exercises.

Lesson Focus -- Long-Rope Jumping Skills

1. Run through turning rope from front door approach.
2. Run through turning rope from back door approach.
3. Try different approaches, a few jumps and varied exits
   a. Run in front door, out back door.
   b. Run in front door and out front door.
   c. Run in back door and out back door.
   d. Run in back door and out front door.
   e. Run in front or back door, jump and do a quarter, half and full turn in the air.
   f. Add individual rope.
   g. Individual choice or with a partner.
4. Hot Pepper: *Gradually* increase the speed of the rope
5. High Water: *Gradually* raise the height of the rope while it is turned.
6. Have more than one child jump at a time. Students can enter in pairs or any other combination. Have jumpers change positions while jumping.
7. Have jumper attempt to jump while holding a beanbag or playground ball between the knees.
8. Have one of the turners jump the long rope.
9. Play catch with a partner while jumping the rope.
10. Egg Beater: Two long ropes are turned simultaneously with four turners.
11. Double Dutch: Requires two long ropes turned alternately. Rope near jumper is turned back door and far rope front door. To start turning, begin with the ropes held tight. Start turning in small circles and gradually move together.

Turning the rope is a difficult skill for young children. It must be practiced regularly until children can maintain an even, steady rhythm. Effective turning is requisite to successful jumping. If turning is not rhythmic, skilled jumpers will have problems. Youngsters must be taught: Learn to turn first, then learn to jump.

Front door means entering from the side where the rope is turning forward and toward the jumper after it reaches its peak. Back door means entering from the side where the rope is turning backward and away from the jumper. To enter front door, the jumper follows the rope in and jumps when it completes the turn. To enter back door, the jumper waits until the rope reaches its peak and moves in as the rope moves downward.

Fly Trap

Supplies: None

Skills: Fundamental locomotor movements

Half of the class is scattered around the playing area, sitting on the floor in cross-legged fashion. These children form the trap. The other children are the flies, and they buzz around the seated children. When a whistle is blown, the flies must freeze where they are. If any of the trappers can touch a fly, that fly sits down at that spot and becomes a trapper. The trappers must keep their seats glued to the floor.

The game continues until all of the flies are caught. Some realism is given to the game if the flies make buzzing sounds and move their arms as wings.

Teaching suggestion: Some experience with the game enables the teacher to determine how far apart to place the seated children. After all (or most) of the flies have been caught, the groups trade places. The method of locomotion should be changed occasionally also.

Trades

Supplies: None

Skills: Imagery, running, dodging

The class is divided into two teams of equal number, each of which has a goal line. One team, the chasers, remains behind its goal line. The other team, the runners, approaches from its goal line, marching to the following dialogue:

Runners: Here we come.

Chasers: Where from?

Runners: New Orleans.

Chasers: What's your trade?

Runners: Lemonade.

Chasers: Show us some.

Runners move up close to the other team's goal line and proceed to act out an occupation or a specific task that they have chosen previously. The opponents try to guess what the pantomime represents. On a correct guess, the running team must run back to its goal line chased by the others. Any runner tagged must join the chasers. The game is repeated with roles reversed. The team ending with the greater number of players is the winner.

Teaching suggestion: If a team has trouble guessing the pantomime, the other team should provide hints. Teams also should be encouraged to have a number of activities selected so that little time is consumed in choosing the next activity to be pantomimed.

Fox Hunt

Supplies: None

Skills: Running, dodging

Two players form trees by facing each other and holding hands. The third member of the group is a fox and stands between the hands of the trees. Three players are identified as foxes without trees and three players are designated as hounds. The hounds try to tag foxes who are not in trees. The extra foxes may move to a tree and displace the fox who is standing in the tree. In addition, the foxes in trees may leave the safety of their trees at any time. If the hound tags a fox, their roles are reversed immediately, the fox becoming the hound.

The game should be stopped at regular intervals to allow the players who are trees to change places with the foxes and hounds. Different locomotor movements can be specified to add variety to the game.

Lesson Plans for Grades 3-4 - Week 8
Manipulative Skills Using Playground Balls

Objectives:
To sequence a series of locomotor movements
To participate in physical activity that exercises all body parts
To throw and catch a playground ball
To control a playground ball with the feet
To appreciate differences in ability among peers

Equipment Required:
Signs and music for circuit training
5-6 hoops
5-6 individual jump ropes
One 8½" playground ball or foam rubber
ball for each student

Instructional Activities	Teaching Hints

Introductory Activity -- Magic Number Challenges

Students are challenged to put together a combination of locomotor movements corresponding to the magic numbers designated (e.g., 10, 8 and 7). Students would have to do three different movements 10, 8 and 7 time, respectively. Use cards with specified numbers. Think of new activities for each series of numbers.

The number of movements, the repetitions and the types of movements can be changed to offer a wide variety of challenges.

Fitness Development Activity –Circuit Training

Place an equal number of students at each station. The following are examples of exercises that can be used at each station.

    Rope Jumping
    Triceps Push-Ups
    Agility Run
    Body Circles
    Hula Hoop
    Knee Touch Curl-Ups
    Crab Walk
    Tortoise and Hare
    Bend and Twist

Tape alternating segments of silence and music to signal duration of exercise. Music segments (begin at 30 seconds) indicate activity at each station while intervals of silence (10 seconds) announce it is time to stop and move forward to the next station.

See text, p. 174-186 for descriptions of exercises.

Conclude circuit training with 2-4 minutes of walking, jogging, rope jumping or other aerobic activity. See text, p. 191-194 for descriptions of circuit training.

Ask students to do the best they can.
Expect workloads to differ.

Lesson Focus -- Manipulative Skills Using Playground Balls

Individual Activities

Controlled rolling and handling
1. Sit, stand, or on back--roll ball around and handle it between legs, behind back to develop a proper "feel" of the ball.

Bounce and catch
1. Two hands, one hand.
2. Bounce at different levels.
3. Bounce between legs.
4. Close eyes and bounce.
5. Dribble ball in a stationary and/or moving position.
6. Dribble and follow the commands, such as: move forward, backward, in a circle, sideways, while walking, galloping, trotting, etc.

Toss and catch
1. Toss and catch, vary height.
2. Add various challenges while tossing (i.e., touch floor, clap hands, turn, make body turns, sit down, lie down).
3. Toss and let bounce. Also add some challenges as above.
4. Toss up and catch behind back--toss from behind back and catch in front.
5. Create moving challenges (i.e., toss, run five steps, catch, toss, back up five hops, and catch).

Give students two or three activities to practice so you have time to move and help youngsters. Alternate activities from each of the categories so students receive a variety of skills to practice.

When catching, soft receipt of the ball is achieved by "giving" with the hands and arms. The hands should reach out somewhat to receive the ball and then cushion the impact by bringing the ball in toward the body in a relaxed way.

Toss high as you can and still maintain control.
To catch a throw above the waist, the hands should be positioned so that the thumbs are together. To receive a throw below the waist, the little fingers should be kept toward each other and the thumbs kept out.

Bat the ball (as in volleyball) to self (teach a low-controlled bat).
1. Bat the ball--use palm, back, and side of hand.
2. Bat the ball using different body parts.

Foot skills
1. Pick the ball up with both feet and catch. Both front and rear of body catch.
2. From a sitting position, ball between feet, toss ball up and catch with hands.
3. While sitting, toss ball up with hands and catch with feet.
4. Put ball between feet or knees and play tag games.
5. Keep ball in air by using feet, knees, head. How many times can you bounce it in succession.

Partner Activities
Passing skills
1. Two-handed, right and left.
2. Throw to various targets--high, low, right and left.
3. Odd throws—under leg, around body, football center, shot-put, windmill, discus.
4. Push-shot types. Straight push, arch.
5. Roll the ball to partner. Flick it in the air with foot and catch.
6. Have one partner dribble and the other attempt to take it away without fouling.

Laterality is an important consideration. Right and left members of the body should be given practice in turn.

When throwing to a partner, unless otherwise specified, the throw should reach the partner at about chest height. At times, different target points should be specified---high, low, right, left, at the knee, and so on.

Distance between partners should be short at first and should be lengthened gradually.

Control the passes. Move closer together if necessary.

Game Activity

Bounce Ball
   Supplies: Volleyballs or rubber playground balls of about the same size
   Skills: Throwing, ball rolling
   The court is divided into halves (30 by 40 ft each). Children form two teams. Each team occupies one half of the court and is given a number of balls. One or two players from each team should be assigned to retrieve balls behind their own end lines. The object of the game is to bounce or roll the ball over the opponents' end line. A ball thrown across the line on a fly does not count.
   Two scorers are needed, one at each end line. Players can move wherever they wish in their own area but cannot cross the centerline. After the starting signal, the balls are thrown back and forth at will.
Variation: A row of benches is placed across the center line. Throws must go over the benches and bounce in the other team's area to score.

One Step
   Supplies: A ball or beanbag for each pair of children
   Skills: Throwing, catching
   Two children stand facing each other about 3 ft apart. One has a ball or a beanbag. The object of the game is to throw or toss the item in the stipulated manner so that the partner can catch it without moving his feet on or from the ground. When the throw is completed successfully, the thrower takes one step backward and waits for the throw from her partner. Children can try to increase their distance to an established line, or the two children who move the greatest distance apart can be declared the winners. Variables to provide interest and challenge are type of throw, type of catch, and kind of step. Throwing can be underhand, overhand, two-handed, under one leg, around the back, and so on. Catching can be two-handed, left-handed, right-handed, to the side, and so on. The step can be a giant step, a tiny step, a hop, a jump, or a similar movement.
   When either child misses, moves the feet, or fails to follow directions, the partners move forward and start over. A double line of children facing each other makes a satisfactory formation.

Lesson Plans for Grades 3-4 - Week 9
Throwing Skills (2)

Objectives:
To cooperatively participate in a simple tag game
To perform continuous fitness activity
To know the elements of proper throwing
To throw with maximum velocity

Equipment Required:
Many types of balls for throwing
Throwing targets; hoops, mats, bowling
    pins and/or cageball
Tape for exercises
Whistle

Instructional Activities	Teaching Hints

Introductory Activity -- Fastest Tag in the West

All students are it. On signal, they try to tag each other. If they are tagged, they must freeze, but they are eligible to tag other students who pass near them. If two or more players tag each other simultaneously, they are both/all "frozen."

The focus of this game is activity. Don't overemphasize rules. When about half of the class is frozen, start the game over.

Fitness Development Activity -- Walk, Trot and Jog

Move to the following signals:
1. One drumbeat - walk.
2. Two drumbeats - trot.
3. Three drumbeats - jog.
4. Whistle - freeze and perform exercises.

Perform various strength and flexibility exercises between bouts of walk, trot and jog. See text, p. 174-186 for descriptions of exercises.
1. Bend and Twist
2. Sitting Stretch
3. Push-Up Challenges
4. Abdominal Challenges
5. Trunk Twister
6. Body Circles
7. Crab Walk

Tape alternating segments of silence and music to signal duration of exercise. Music segments indicate aerobic activity (30-45 seconds) while intervals of silence announce flexibility and strength development activities (30 seconds).

Assure that students run under control (not as fast as they can). Run in the same direction around the area.

Allow students to perform at a level they feel comfortable. Youngsters are genetically different and should not be expected to do the same amount of exercise repetitions.

Lesson Focus -- Throwing Skills (2)

Review and practice throwing for form
1. Review proper throwing form outlined in Lesson 3 (p. 5).
    a. Throw yarn balls from a standing position 20 feet from the wall. Throw five balls, retrieve and repeat.
    b. Throw yarn balls or tennis balls using the proper grip. Throw at bowling pins or hoops leaning against the wall and encourage trying to knock down the hoops.. Throw from a distance of 20 to 25 feet depending on skill level. Gradually increase the distance from the wall.

Review and practice throwing for velocity
1. Review throwing for velocity in Lesson 3 (p. 6). Set up activities using large targets so students will throw forcefully.
    a. Throw at mats on the wall. Throw tennis balls hard from 16 to 20 feet. Retrieve only if the balls roll beyond the throwing line.
    b. Throw at hoops leaning against mats on the wall.
    c. Large target throw. Use a circle or square 4 feet in diameter placed on the wall. Students should throw from 20 to 35 feet.

Practice throwing at targets
1. Use targets to increase motivation. The targets should encourage throwing for velocity rather than accuracy. Some examples of targets are:
    a. Throw through hoops suspended from basketball goals.
    b. Use large boxes for targets and try to throw inside the box. Try throwing at the side of the box. Throw at holes cut in the sides of the box.

Throwing takes a great deal of practice to master. Two major issues to consider when teaching throwing are:
1. How can I arrange my class so students receive the most opportunity to throw?
2. How can I arrange my class so students get to throw with maximum velocity. A mature pattern of throwing cannot be learned if students are not allowed to throw with maximum force.

Proper form and velocity of throws are closely related. A reason for practicing form is to encourage students to think about technique.

Give each student 4 or 5 balls to throw. On signal, when all the balls have been thrown students go retrieve the same number of balls they have thrown.

Throwing for targets is exciting for youngsters. It can also increase the motivational level of the lesson.

d. Cageball throw. Throwers try to move it into the corner by throwing at it.

e. Many bowling pins set near the walls.

f. Graduated-size target throw. Use a large concentric circle (or square) with 4 feet, 3 feet and 2 feet diameter circles.

Game Activity

In the Prison

Supplies: 15-20 throwing balls

Skill: Throwing

Two teams, one assigned to each half of the gym. Balls (15-20) are placed on the center line. On signal, each team throws the balls to the other side of the gym. The object of the game is to get all the balls into the other team's backcourt area (or prison) which extends 10 feet from the wall. The teacher stops play by blowing a whistle, then counting the number of balls in the "prison."

Snowball

Supplies: 36 yarn balls

Skill: Throwing

Two teams, one assigned to each half of the gym. Each student has a yarn ball. Players can be hit three times. Each time they are hit they call out the number (1, 2, 3) of times they have been hit. After the third hit they must go to the side of the area and count to 25 before they can reenter. Teams must stay in their half of the gym.

Center Target Throw

Supplies: 20 - 8" gray foam balls and 20 bowling pins

Skill: Throwing

The area is divided into quadrants. Two teams compete, and each team has its own set of targets (bowling pins) set on a center line. Half of each team is placed in opposing quadrants with the pins in the middle. Team A, on the left half of the area, has players on both sides of the center line behind restraining lines 15 to 20 feet away from the center target line. Team B is positioned the same way on the right half of the area. Each team tries to knock down all of its bowling pins as quickly as possible.

Target Ball Throw

Supplies: 10 - 18" beachballs and 36 yarn balls

Skill: Throwing

Beachballs are placed on the center line of the gym. There are two teams and each must stay in its half of the gym. Players have yarn balls. The object of the game is to roll the beachballs into the other team's court by hitting them with the yarn balls. The team that has the least number of beachballs on its side when the teacher blows the whistle is the winner.

Lesson Plans for Grades 3-4 - Week 10
Walking and Jogging Skills

Objectives:
To travel throughout the area and be able to avoid or catch another individual
To understand the differences in aerobic capacities among classmates
To find a running or walking pace that is comfortable for an extended time

Equipment Required:
Recreational and individual equipment desired
Tom-tom and exercise tape for fitness

Instructional Activities	Teaching Hints
Introductory Activity -- Group Tag	
A number of players are designated to be it. On signal, they try to tag other players. If a player is tagged, that player becomes it and must try to tag another. In other words, each person who is it tags only one player. If players want to be "safe," they must stand toe-to-toe in a group of three or more students.	Encourage students to say "you're it" when they tag someone. If students can't catch someone, they can give up being it.
Fitness Development Activity -- Walk, Trot, and Jog	
Move to the following signals: 1. One drumbeat - walk. 2. Two drumbeats - trot. 3. Three drumbeats - jog. 4. Whistle - freeze and perform exercises. Perform various strength and flexibility exercises between bouts of walk, trot and jog. See text, p. 174-186 for descriptions of exercises. 1. Bend and Twist 2. Sitting Stretch 3. Push-Up Challenges 4. Abdominal Challenges 5. Trunk Twister 6. Body Circles 7. Crab Walk	Tape alternating segments of silence and music to signal duration of exercise. Music segments indicate aerobic activity (30-45 seconds) while intervals of silence announce flexibility and strength development activities (30 seconds). Assure that students run under control (not as fast as they can) and in the same direction. Allow students to perform at a level they feel comfortable. Youngsters are genetically different and should not be expected to do the same amount of exercise repetitions.

Lesson Focus -- Walking and Jogging Skills

The walking and jogging lesson should be a relaxed lesson with emphasis on developing activity patterns that can be used outside of the school environment. An educational approach to this lesson teaches students that walking and jogging are done without equipment and offer excellent health benefits. It is an activity that can literally be done for a lifetime. The following are suggestions for implementing this unit of instruction:

1. Youngsters should be allowed to find a friend with whom they want to jog or walk. The result is usually a friend of similar ability level. A way to judge correct pace is to be able to talk with a friend without undue stress. If students are too winded to talk, they are probably running too fast. A selected friend will encourage talking and help assure that the experience is positive and within the student's aerobic capacity. *Pace, not race* is the motto.

2. Jogging and walking should be done in any desired direction so others are unable to keep track of the distance covered. Doing laps on a track is one of the surest ways to discourage less able youngsters. They always finish last and are open to chiding by the rest of the class.

3. Jogging and walking should be done for a specified time rather than a specified distance. All youngsters should not have to run the same distance. This goes against the philosophy of accompanying individual differences and varying aerobic capacities. Running or walking for a set amount of time will allow the less able child to move without fear of ridicule.

4. Teachers should not be concerned about foot action, since the child selects naturally the means that is most comfortable. Arm movement should be easy and natural, with elbows bent. The head and upper body should be held up and back. The eyes look ahead. The general body position in walking and jogging should be erect but relaxed.

5. Jogging and walking should not be a competitive, timed activity. Each youngster should move at a self-determined pace. Racing belongs in the track program. Another reason to avoid speed is that racing keeps youngsters from learning to pace themselves. For developing endurance and gaining health benefits, it is more important to move for a longer time at a slower speed than to run at top speed for a shorter distance.

6. It is motivating for many youngsters to run with a piece of equipment, i.e., beanbag or jump rope. They can play catch with a beanbag or roll a hoop while walking or jogging.

Game Activity -- Individual or Recreational Activity

When youngsters are finished jogging, allow them the opportunity to participate in a choice of individual or recreational activities.

Lesson Plans for Grades 3-4 - Week 11
Rhythmic Movement (1)

Objectives:
To perform a locomotor movement and manipulate an object simultaneously
To perform rhythmic movements in folk dances
To appreciate the origin of folk dances
To understand the cultural differences among students from different backgrounds

Equipment Required:
Tom-tom and exercise tape for fitness
Music for games
Music for rhythmic activities
6 cones and 6 pinnies

Instructional Activities	Teaching Hints

Introductory Activity -- Locomotor and Manipulative Activity

Each child is given a bean bag and moves around the area using various basic locomotor movements. Students toss and catch their beanbags while moving. On signal, they drop the beanbags and jump and/or hop over as many bags as possible.

Vary the challenge by specifying the number or color of beanbags to move over or around.

Fitness Development Activity -- Walk, Trot, and Jog

Move to the following signals:
1. One drumbeat - walk.
2. Two drumbeats - trot.
3. Three drumbeats - jog.
4. Whistle - freeze and perform exercises.

Perform various strength and flexibility exercises between bouts of walk, trot and jog. See text, p. 174-186 for descriptions of exercises.
1. Bend and Twist
2. Sitting Stretch
3. Push-Up Challenges
4. Abdominal Challenges
5. Trunk Twister
6. Body Circles
7. Crab Walk

Tape alternating segments of silence and music to signal duration of exercise. Music segments indicate aerobic activity (30-45 seconds) while intervals of silence announce flexibility and strength development activities (30 seconds).

Assure that students run under control (not as fast as they can).

Allow students to perform at a level they feel comfortable. Youngsters are genetically different and should not be expected to do the same amount of exercise repetitions.

Lesson Focus -- Rhythmic Movement (1)

Make dances easy for students to learn by implementing some of the following techniques:
Rhythms should be taught like other sport skills. Avoid striving for perfection so students know it is acceptable to make mistakes. Teach a variety of dances rather than one or two in depth in case some students find it difficult to master a specific dance.
1. Teach the dances without using partners.
2. Allow youngsters to move in any direction without left-right orientation.
3. Use scattered formation instead of circles.
4. Emphasize strong movements such as clapping and stamping to increase involvement.
5. Play the music at a slower speed when first learning the dance.
When introducing a dance, use the following methodology:
1. Tell about the dance and listen to the music.
2. Clap the beat and learn the verse.
3. Practice the dance steps without the music and with verbal cues.
4. Practice the dance with the music.
Records can be ordered from Wagon Wheel Records, 17191 Corbina Lane #203, Huntington Beach, CA (714) 846-8169.

The Bird Dance (Chicken Dance)

Records: AD-831; ESP 001
Formation: Circle or scatter formation, partners facing
Directions:

Measures	Part I Action
1	Four snaps---thumb and fingers, hands up
2	Four flaps---arms up and down, elbows bent
3	Four wiggles---hips, knees bent low
4	Four claps
5--16	Repeat action of measures 1--4 three times

Measures	Part II Action
1—8	With a partner, either do a right-hand star with 16 skips or 16 walking steps, or do an elbow swing. (Skip, 2, 3, . . . 15, change hands)
9—16	Repeat with the left hand. On the last four counts of the last swing, everyone changes partners. If dancing in a circle formation, partners B advance forward counter-clockwise to the next partner A. If dancing in a scattered formation, everyone scrambles to find a new partner. (Skip, 2, 3, . . . 12, change partners)

Csebogar (Hungarian)

Records: LS E-15; MAV 1042
Formation: Single circle, partners facing center, hands joined with partners B on the right
Directions:

Measures	Part I Action
1--4	Take seven slides to the left. (Slide, 2, 3, 4, 5, 6, 7, change)
5--8	Take seven slides to the right. (Back, 2, 3, 4, 5, 6, 7, stop)
9—12	Take three skips to the center and stamp on the fourth beat. Take three skips backward to place and stamp on the eighth beat. (Forward, 2, 3, stamp; Backward, 2, 3, stamp)
13--16	Hook right elbows with partner and turn around twice in place, skipping. (Swing, 2, 3, 4, 5, 6, 7, 8)

Measures	Part II Action (Partners face each other in a single circle with hands joined.)
17--20	Holding both of partner's hands, take four draw steps (step, close) toward the center of the circle. (Step-close, 2-close, 3-close, 4-close)
21--24	Take four draw steps back to place. (Step-close, 2-close, 3-close, 4-close)
25--26	Go toward the center of the circle with two draw steps. (In-close, 2-close)
27--28	Take two draw steps back to place. (Out-close, 2-close)
29--32	Hook elbows and repeat the elbow swing, finishing with a shout and facing the center of the circle in the original formation. (Swing, 2, 3, 4, 5, "Csebogar")

Teddy Bear Mixer (American)

Record: LS E-11
Formation: Double circle of couples facing counterclockwise, partner B on right side of partner A, inside hands joined. Walking step is used throughout.
Directions:

Measures	Action
1—2	Starting with partner A's left foot (B's right), walk three steps in the line of direction and pause. (Walk, 2, 3, pause)
3—4	Starting with A's right foot (B's left), walk backwards three steps in the reverse line of direction and pause. (Back, 2, 3, pause)
5—6	Starting on the left foot, As move three steps toward the center of the circle and pause. Starting on the right foot, Bs move away from the center of the circle three steps and pause. At the completion of the third step, a handclap may be used during the pause. (Separate, 2, 3, pause)
7—8	Starting on A's right foot (B's left), both move toward each other, rejoining inside hands. (Together, 2, 3, pause)
9—10	Repeat measures 1 and 2. (Walk, 2, 3, pause)
11--12	Repeat measures 3 and 4. (Back, 2, 3, pause)
13--14	Repeat measures 5 and 6. (Separate, 2, 3, pause)
15--16	Starting with A's right foot (B's left), both move together diagonally, with A moving forward to the B ahead to acquire a new partner for the next repetition. (Diagonally, 2, 3, pause)

Crested Hen (Danish)

Records: HLP 4027; MAV 1042
Formation: Sets of three. One child is designated the center child.
Directions:

Measures	Part I Action
1—4	Dancers in each set form a circle. Starting with a stamp with the left foot, each set circles to the left, using step-hops. (Stamp and, 2 and, 3 and, 4 and, 5 and, 6 and, 7 and, stop)
5—8	The figure is repeated. Dancers reverse direction, beginning again with a stamp with the left foot and following with step-hops. The change of direction should be vigorous and definite, with the left foot crossing over the right. At the end of the sequence, two dancers release each other's hands to break the circle and stand on either side of the center person, forming a line of three while retaining joined hands with the center dancer. (Stamp and, 2 and, 3 and, 4 and, 5 and, 6 and, 7 and, line)

Measures	Part II Action (During this part, the dancers use the step-hop continuously while making the pattern figures)
9—10	The dancer on the right moves forward in an arc to the left and dances under the arch formed by the other two. (Under and, 2 and, 3 and, 4 and)
11—12	After the right dancer has gone through, the two forming the arch turn under (dishrag), to form once again a line of three. (Turn and, 2 and, 3 and, 4 and)
13—16	The dancer on the left then repeats the pattern, moving forward in an arc under the arch formed by the other two, who turn under to unravel the line. (Under and, 2 and, 3 and, 4 and; Turn and, 2 and, 3 and, circle)

As soon as Part II is completed, dancers again join hands in a small circle. The entire dance is repeated. Another of the three can be designated the center dancer.

Game Activity

Whistle March

Supplies: Music

Skill: Moving rhythmically

A record with a brisk march is needed. Children are scattered around the room, individually walking in various directions and keeping time to the music. A whistle is blown a number of times. At this signal, lines are formed of that precise number of children, no more and no fewer. To form the lines, children stand side by side with locked elbows. As soon as a line of the proper number is formed, it begins to march to the music counterclockwise around the room. Any children left over go to the center of the room and remain there until the next signal. On the next whistle signal (a single blast), the lines break up, and all walk individually around the room in various directions.

When forming a new line, make a rule that children may not form the same combinations as in the previous line.

Arches

Supplies: Music

Skills: Moving rhythmically

The game is similar to London Bridge. An arch is placed in the playing area. (To form an arch, two players stand facing one another with hands joined and arms raised.) When the music starts, the other players move in a circle, passing under the arch. Suddenly, the music stops, and the arch is brought down by dropping the hands. All players caught in an arch immediately pair off to form other arches, keeping in a general circle formation. If a caught player does not have a partner, he waits in the center of the circle until one is available. The last players caught (or left) form arches for the next game.

The arches should be warned not to bring down their hands and arms too forcefully so that children passing under are not pummeled.

Variation: Different types of music can be used, and children can move according to the pattern of the music.

Home Base

Supplies: Cones to delineate the area, four pinnies

Skills: Reaction time, locomotor movements, body management

The area is divided into four quadrants with cones or floor lines. Each quadrant is the home base for one of the squads. The captain of the squad wears a pinnie for easy identification. The teams begin in a straight line sitting on the floor. The teacher calls out a locomotor movement which the players use to move throughout the area. When the teacher calls "Home base," the students return to their quadrant and return to the starting position behind their captain. The first team to return to proper position (sitting in a straight line) is awarded 2 points. Second place receives 1 point.

Teaching suggestion: Avoid calling "Home base" until the students have left the area of their quadrant. A number of different formations can be specified which students must assume upon return to their home base.

Lesson Plans for Grades 3-4 - Week 12
Hockey-Related Activities (1)

Objectives:
To understand and translate into movement the concepts of level, direction and size
To demonstrate how the hockey stick should be handled for safety
To practice passing and fielding a hockey puck
To design drills for practicing hockey skills

Equipment Required:
Exercise tape
One puck and hockey stick for each
    student
Tumbling mats for goals

Instructional Activities	Teaching Hints

Introductory Activity -- Movement Varieties

Move using a basic locomotor movement. Then add variety to the movement by asking students to respond to the following factors:
1. Level--low, high, in-between.
2. Direction--straight, zigzag, circular, curved, forward, backward, upward, downward.
3. Size--large, tiny, medium movements.

Help students understand the concepts of level, direction, and size by briefly discussing them.

Encourage creativity by reinforcing novel responses.

Fitness Development Activity -- Astronaut Drills

Walk while doing Arm circles	30 seconds
Crab Alternate-Leg Extension	35 seconds
Skip	30 seconds
Body Twist	35 seconds
Slide	30 seconds
Jumping Jack variations	35 seconds
Crab Walk to center and back	30 seconds
Abdominal Challenges	35 seconds
Hop to center and back	30 seconds
Push-Up Challenges	35 seconds
Gallop	30 seconds
Bear Hugs	35 seconds
Pogo Stick Jump	30 seconds

Cool down with stretching and walking or jogging for 1-2 minutes.

See text, p. 174-186 for descriptions of exercises.

Tape alternating segments of silence (35 seconds) and music (30 seconds) to signal duration of exercise. Music segments indicate aerobic activity while intervals of silence announce flexibility and strength development activities.

Emphasize quality movement over quantity. Allow students to adjust the workload pace. They should be able to exercise at a pace that is consistent with their personal fitness level.

See text, p. 163-167 for descriptions of challenges.

Lesson Focus -- Hockey-Related Activities (1)

Skills
Practice the following skills:
1. Gripping and carrying the stick.
   The hockey stick should be held with both hands and carried as low to the ground as possible. The basic grip puts the left hand at the top of the stick and the right hand 6 to 12 inches below the left.

To ensure accuracy as well as safety, the stick must not be swung above waist height.

2. Controlled Dribble.
   The controlled dribble consists of a series of short taps in the direction in which the player chooses to move. The hands should be spread 10 to 14 inches apart to gain greater control of the stick. As the player becomes more skilled, the hands can be moved closer together. The stick is turned so that the blade faces the ball. The grip should not be changed, but rather, the hands should be rotated until the back of the left hand and the palm of the right hand face the ball. The ball can then be tapped just far enough in front of the player to keep it away from the feet but not more than one full stride away from the stick.

Dribbling instructional cues:
1. Control the puck. It should always be within reach of the stick.
2. Hold the stick firmly.
3. Keep the elbows away from the body.

3. Front Field.
   For the front field, the student must keep an eye on the ball, move to a point in line with its path, and extend the flat side of the blade forward to meet the ball. The faster the ball approaches, the more she must learn to give with the stick to absorb the momentum of the ball. The player should field the ball in front of the body and not permit it to get too close.

Front fielding instructional cues:
1. Field with a "soft stick." This means holding the stick with relaxed hands.
2. Allow the puck to hit the stick and then "give" to make a soft reception.
3. Keep the hands apart on the stick.

4. Forehand Pass.

The forehand pass is a short pass that usually occurs from the dribble. It should be taught before driving, because the quick hit requires accuracy rather than distance. The player spreads the feet with toes pointed slightly forward when striking. Approach the ball with the stick held low and bring the stick straight back, in line with the intended direction of the hit. The hands should be the same distance apart as in the carrying position, and the stick should be lifted no higher than waist level. The player's right hand guides the stick down and through the ball. The head should be kept down with the eyes on the ball. A short follow-through occurs after contact.

Drills
Use the following drills to practice the skills above:
1. Dribbling
   a. Each student has a stick and ball. On signal, change directions while maintaining control of the ball.
   b. Dribble and dodge imaginary tacklers or dodge around a set of cones. Partners may act as tacklers.
   c. Students in pairs--20 feet apart. One partner dribbles toward the other, goes around him or her, and returns to starting point. The first student then drives the ball to the second, who completes the same sequence.
2. Forehand Passing and Front Fielding
   a. From 8 to 10 feet apart, partners forehand pass and front field the ball back and forth to each other both from moving and stationary positions.
   b. Partners 20 feet apart--players pass the ball back and forth with emphasis on *fielding* and *immediately* hitting the ball back.

Forehand passing instructional cues:
1. Approach the puck with the side facing the direction of the pass.
2. Keep the head down and eyes on the puck.
3. Keep the stick below waist level at all times.
4. Drive the stick through the puck.

Hockey is a rough game when children are not taught the proper methods of stick handling. They need to be reminded often to use caution and good judgment when handling hockey sticks.

Ample equipment increases individual practice time and facilitates skill development. A stick and a ball or puck for each child are desirable.

If hockey is played on a gym floor, a plastic puck or yarn ball should be used. If played on a carpeted area or outdoors, a whiffle ball is used. An 8-foot folding mat set on end makes a satisfactory goal.

Game Activity -- Hockey Lead-Up Games

Circle Keep-Away
Supplies: One stick per person, a puck or ball
Skills: Passing, fielding
Players are spaced evenly around the circle, with one player in the center. The object of the game is to keep the player in the center from touching the puck. The puck is passed back and forth, with emphasis on accurate passing and fielding. If the player in the center touches the puck, the player who last passed the puck takes the place of the center player. A change of players also can be made after a passing or fielding error.

Star Wars Hockey
Supplies: One stick per player, four pucks or balls
Skill: Dribbling
Each team forms one side of a square. Each side is numbered so that there are four players with the same number (one from each side of the square).
1. Four pucks (or balls) are used. When a number is called, players with that number go to a puck and dribbles it out of the square through the spot previously occupied, around the square counterclockwise, and back to the original spot. Circles 12 in. in diameter are drawn on the floor to provide a definite place to which the puck must be returned. If the game is played outdoors, hoops can mark the spot to which the puck must be returned.
2. No player is permitted to use anything other than the stick in making the circuit and returning the puck to the inside of the hoop. The penalty for infractions is disqualification.

Lane Hockey
Supplies: Hockey stick per player, puck, two goals
Skills: All hockey skills
The field is divided into eight lanes. A defensive and an offensive player are placed in each of the eight lanes. A goalkeeper for each team is also positioned in front of the goal area. Players may not leave their lane during play. A shot on goal may not be taken until a minimum of two passes have been completed. This rule encourages looking for teammates and passing to someone in a better position before a shot on goal is taken.

Players should be encouraged to maintain their spacing during play. The purpose of the lanes is to force them to play a zone rather than rushing to the puck. A free hit (unguarded) is awarded a team if a foul occurs. Players should be rotated after a goal is scored or at regular time intervals.

Variation: Increase the number of lanes to five or six. This involves a larger number of players. On a large playing area, the lanes may be broken into thirds rather than halves. Increase the number of passes that should be made prior to a shot on goal.

Circle Hockey Straddleball

Supplies: Hockey sticks and pucks or yarnballs

Skills: Passing and fielding

Children are in circle formation, facing in. Each player stands in a wide straddle stance two or three feet apart. The object of the game is to pass one of the pucks between the legs of another. Each time a puck goes between the legs of an individual, a point is scored. The players having the fewest points scored against them are winners. Keep the circles small so students have more opportunities to handle the puck.

Lesson Plans for Grades 3-4 - Week 13
Hockey-Related Activities (2)

Objectives:
To practice passing and fielding a hockey puck
To design drills for practicing hockey skills
To understand and perform goaltending skills

Equipment Required:
Hockey sticks and pucks or yarn balls
Cones
Music for exercises
Tumbling mats for goals

Instructional Activities	Teaching Hints

Introductory Activity -- New Leader

Make groups of 3-4 students, assigning one of the students to be a leader. The groups move around the area, following the leader. On signal, the last person moves to the head of the squad and become the leader. Various types of locomotor movements and/or exercises should be used.

Movement should be continuous unless an exercise is being performed.

Design personal movement patterns

Fitness Development Activity -- Astronaut Drills

Walk while doing Arm circles	30 seconds	Tape alternating segments of silence (30 seconds) and music (35 seconds) to signal duration of exercise. Music segments indicate aerobic activity while intervals of silence announce flexibility and strength development activities.
Crab Alternate-Leg Extension	35 seconds	
Skip	30 seconds	
Body Twist	35 seconds	
Slide	30 seconds	
Jumping Jack variations	35 seconds	
Crab Walk to center and back	30 seconds	
Abdominal Challenges	35 seconds	Use scatter formation; ask students to change directions from time to time in order to keep spacing.
Hop to center and back	30 seconds	
Push-Up Challenges	35 seconds	
Gallop	30 seconds	
Bear Hugs	35 seconds	Allow students to adjust the workload pace.
Pogo Stick Jump	30 seconds	

Cool down with stretching and walking or jogging for 1-2 minutes.

See text, p. 174-186 for descriptions of exercises.

See text, p. 163-167 for descriptions of challenges.

Lesson Focus -- Hockey-Related Activities (2)

Skills:

Review and practice skills introduced last week:
1. Gripping and carrying the stick
2. Controlled dribble
3. Front field
4. Forehand Pass

Introduce new skills:
1. Driving.

    Driving is used to hit the ball moderate to long distances and to shoot at the goal. It differs from other passes in that the hands are brought together more toward the end of the stick. This gives the leverage necessary to apply greater force to the ball and results in more speed and greater distance. The swing and hit are similar to the quick hit. Stick control should be stressed so that wild swinging does not occur.

2. Tackling

    The tackle is a means of taking the ball away from an opponent. The tackler moves toward the opponent with the stick held low. The tackle is timed so that the blade of the stick is placed against the ball when the ball is off the opponent's stick. The tackler then quickly dribbles or passes in the direction of the goal. Throwing the stick or striking carelessly at the ball should be discouraged. Players need to remember that a successful tackle is not always possible.

3. Goalkeeping

    The goalie may kick the ball, stop it with any part of the body, or allow it to rebound off the body or hand. He may not, however, hold the ball or throw it toward the other end of the playing area. The goalkeeper is positioned in front of the goal line and moves between the goal posts. When a ball is hit toward the goal, the goalie should attempt to move in front of the ball and to keep his feet together. This allows the body to block the ball should the stick miss it. After the block, the ball is passed immediately to a teammate.

Review the drills presented last week:
1. Dribbling
2. Forehand Passing and Front Fielding

Introduce new drills:

Passing and Fielding drills

    1. The shuttle turn-back drill, in which two files of four or five players face each other, can be used. The first person in the file passes to the first person in the other file, who in turn fields the ball and returns the pass. Each player, when finished, goes to the end of the file.

    2. The downfield drill for passing and fielding skills for on the move. Three files of players start at one end of the field. One player from each file proceeds downfield, passing to and fielding from the others until the other end of the field is reached. A goal shot can be made at this point. The players should remain close together for short passes until a high level of skill is reached.

    3. Practice driving for distance and accuracy with a partner.

Dodging and Tackling Drills

    1. Players spread out on the field, each with a ball. On command, they dribble left, right, forward, and backward. On the command "Dodge," the players dodge an imaginary tackler. Players should concentrate on ball control and dodging in all directions.

    2. Players work in pairs. One partner dribbles toward the other, who attempts to make a tackle. If the tackle is successful, roles are reversed. This drill should be practiced at moderate speeds in the early stages of skill development.

Game Activity -- Hockey Lead-up Games

Modified Hockey

    Supplies: One stick per person, a puck or ball

    Skills: Dribbling, passing, dodging, tackling, face-off

    The teams may take any position on the field as long as they remain inside the boundaries. The object of the game is to hit the puck through the opponent's goal. No goalies are used. At the start of the game and after each score, play begins with a face-off. Each goal is worth one point.

Teaching suggestion: The distance between goal lines is flexible but should be on the long side. If making goals is too easy or too difficult, the width of the goals can be adjusted accordingly.

Lane Hockey

    Supplies: Hockey stick per player, puck, two goals

    Skills: All hockey skills

    The field is divided into eight lanes. A defensive and an offensive player are placed in each of the eight lanes. A goalkeeper for each team is also positioned in front of the goal area. Players may not leave their lane during play. A shot on goal may not be taken until a minimum of two passes have been completed. This rule encourages looking for teammates and passing to someone in a better position before a shot on goal is taken.

    Players should be encouraged to maintain their spacing during play. The purpose of the lanes is to force them to play a zone rather than rushing to the puck. A free hit (unguarded) is awarded a team if a foul occurs. Players should be rotated after a goal is scored or at regular time intervals.

Variation: Increase the number of lanes to five or six. This involves a larger number of players. On a large playing area, the lanes may be broken into thirds rather than halves. Increase the number of passes that should be made prior to a shot on goal.

Lesson Plans for Grades 3-4 - Week 14
Individual Rope Jumping Skills

Objectives:
To be able to jump slow and fast time with a self-turned rope
To identify safety considerations for fast-moving games
To maintain continuous fitness activity

Equipment Required:
Jump rope for each student
Music for exercises
Beanbag and beachballs for games

Instructional Activities	Teaching Hints

Introductory Activity -- Group Over and Under

One half of the class is scattered. Each is in a curled position. The other half of the class leap or jump over the down children. On signal, reverse the group quickly. In place of a curl, the down children can bridge and the other go under.

The down children can also alternate between curl and bridge, as well as move around the area while in a bridged position.

Fitness Development Activity -- Astronaut Drills

Walk while doing Arm circles	30 seconds
Crab Alternate-Leg Extension	35 seconds
Skip	30 seconds
Body Twist	35 seconds
Slide	30 seconds
Jumping Jack variations	35 seconds
Crab Walk to center and back	30 seconds
Abdominal Challenges	35 seconds
Hop to center and back	30 seconds
Push-Up Challenges	35 seconds
Gallop	30 seconds
Bear Hugs	35 seconds
Pogo Stick Jump	30 seconds

Cool down with stretching and walking or jogging for 1-2 minutes.

See text, p. 174-186 for descriptions of exercises.

Tape alternating segments of silence (35 seconds) and music (30 seconds) to signal duration of exercise. Music segments indicate aerobic activity while intervals of silence announce flexibility and strength development activities.

Use scatter formation; ask students to change directions from time to time in order to keep spacing.

Allow students to adjust the workload pace. They should be allowed to move at a space that is consistent with their ability level.

Lesson Focus -- Individual Rope Jumping Skills

1. For students who are having trouble jumping the rope, try some of the following activities:
   a. Jump in place to a tom-tom beat without rope.
   b. Hold both ends of the jump rope in one hand (practice with right and left hands) and turn it to the side so a steady rhythm can be made through a consistent turn. Just before the rope hits the ground, the student should practice jumping.
   c. Start jumping the rope one turn at a time--gradually increase the number of turns.
2. Introduce the two basic jump rhythms:
   a. Slow-time rhythm. In slow time rhythm, the performer jumps the rope and then takes a second jump while the rope is overhead. The jump while the rope is overhead is usually a small, light rebound jump. In slow time, the rope make one full turn for each two jumps.
   b. Fast time rhythm. In fast time rhythm, the student jumps the rope with every jump. The rope makes one full turn for every jump.
3. Introduce some of the basic step variations. The basic steps can be done in slow or fast time.
   a. Side Swing. Swing the rope, held with both hands to one side of the body. Switch and swing the rope on the other side of the body.
   b. Double Side Swing and Jump. Swing the rope once on each side of the body. Follow the second swing with a jump over the rope. The sequence should be swing, swing, jump.

The length of the rope is dependent on the height of the jumper. It should be long enough so that the ends reach to the armpits or slightly higher when the child stands on its center. Grades 3-4 students need mostly 8-foot ropes, with a few 7- and 9-foot lengths. Ropes or handles can be color-coded for length.

Two types of ropes are available; the beaded (plastic segment) and the plastic (licorice) rope. The beaded ropes are heavier and seem easier to turn for beginning jumpers. The drawback to the beaded ropes is that they hurt when they hit another student. Also, if the segments are made round, the rope will roll easily on the floor children may fall when they step on it. The plastic licorice ropes are lighter and give less wind resistance.

c. Alternate-Foot Basic Step. In the Alternate-Foot Basic Step, as the rope passes under the feet, the weight is shifted alternately from one foot to the other, raising the unweighted foot in a running position.

d. Bird Jumps. Jump with the toes pointed in (pigeon walk) and with the toes pointed out (duck walk). Alternate toes in and toes out.

e. Swing-Step Forward. The Swing-Step Forward is the same as the Alternate-Foot Basic Step, except that the free leg swings forward. The knee is kept loose and the foot swings naturally.

f. Rocker Step. In executing the Rocker Step, one leg is always forward in a walking-stride position. As the rope passes under the feet, the weight is shifted from the back foot to the forward foot. The rebound is taken on the forward foot while the rope is above the head. On the next turn of the rope, the weight is shifted from the forward foot to the back foot, repeating the rebound on the back foot.

4. Individual Rope Jumping with a Partner. One student turns and jumps the rope while her partner enters and jumps simultaneously. Entering is sometimes difficult for beginners, so it may be necessary to begin in position and then start turning the rope. The following are some challenges partners can try:

a. Run in and face partner, and both jump.

b. Run in and turn back to partner, and both jump.

c. Decide which steps are to be done; then run in and match steps.

d. Repeat with the rope turning backward.

Instructional cues to use for improving jumping technique are as follows:

a. Keep the arms at the side of the body while turning. (Many children lift the arms to shoulder level trying to move the rope overhead. This makes it impossible for the youngster to jump over the elevated rope.)

b. Turn the rope by making small circles with the wrists.

c. Jump on the balls of the feet.

d. Bend the knees slightly to absorb the force of the jump.

e. Don't jump too high. Make a small jump over the rope.

Game Activity

Follow Me

Supplies: A marker for each child (squares of cardboard or plywood can be used; individual mats or beanbags work well)

Skills: All locomotor movements, stopping

Children are arranged in a rough circle, each standing or sitting with one foot on a marker. An extra player is the guide. He moves around the circle, pointing at different players and asking them to follow. Each player chosen falls in behind the guide. The guide then takes the group on a tour, and the members of the group perform just as the guide does. The guide may hop, skip, do stunts, or execute other movements, and children following must do likewise. At the signal "Home," all run for places with a marker. One child is left without a marker. This child chooses another guide.

Teaching suggestions: Making the last child the new leader is not a good idea, because this causes some children to lag and try to be last. Another way to overcome the tendency to lag is to make the first one back the guide. The teacher can also use a special marker; the first one to this marker becomes the new leader. A penalty can be imposed on the one who does not find a marker.

Trades

Supplies: None

Skills: Imagery, running, dodging

The class is divided into two teams of equal number, each of which has a goal line. One team, the chasers, remains behind its goal line. The other team, the runners, approaches from its goal line, marching to the following dialogue:

Runners: Here we come.

Chasers: Where from?

Runners: New Orleans.

Chasers: What's your trade?

Runners: Lemonade.

Chasers: Show us some.

Runners move up close to the other team's goal line and proceed to act out an occupation or a specific task that they have chosen previously. The opponents try to guess what the pantomime represents. On a correct guess, the running team must run back to its goal line chased by the others. Any runner tagged must join the chasers. The game is repeated with roles reversed. The team ending with the greater number of players is the winner.

Teaching suggestion: If a team has trouble guessing the pantomime, the other team should provide hints. Teams also should be encouraged to have a number of activities selected so that little time is consumed in choosing the next activity to be pantomimed.

Beachball Batball

Supplies: Four to six beachballs

Skills: Batting, tactile handling

Two games are played across the gymnasium area. The teams are scattered throughout the area without restriction as to where they may move. To begin the game, the balls are placed on the centerline dividing the court area. Four to six beachballs are in play at the same time. A score occurs when the beachball is batted over the end line. Once the ball moves across the end line it is dead. Players concentrate on the remaining balls in play.

If a ball is on the floor, it is picked up and batted into play. At no time may a ball be carried. After all four balls are scored, the game ends. A new game is started after teams switch goals.

Lesson Plans for Grades 3-4 - Week 15
Stunts and Tumbling Skills (1)

Objectives:
To jump rope and understand the aerobic value of rope jumping
To support the body weight in a variety of tumbling and stunt activities
To control the body weight in a variety of tumbling and stunt activities
To enjoy participation in group games

Equipment Required:
One jump rope for each child
Music for Continuity Drills
Tumbling mats
Balls for game activities
Bowling pins

Instructional Activities	Teaching Hints

Introductory Activity -- Addition Tag

Two couples are it, and each stands with inside hands joined. These are the taggers. The other children run individually. The couples move around the playground, trying to tag with the free hands. The first person tagged joins the couple, making a trio. The three then chase until they catch a fourth. Once a fourth person is caught, the four divide and form two couples, adding another set of taggers to the game. This continues until all children are tagged.

The game moves faster if started with two couples.

A tag is legal only when the couple or group of three keeps their hands joined.

Fitness Development Activity -- Continuity Drills

Rope Jumping - Forward	30 seconds
Double Crab Kick	45 seconds
Rope Jumping - Backward	30 seconds
Knee Touch Curl-Up	45 seconds
Jump and Slowly Turn Body	30 seconds
Push-Up Challenges	45 seconds
Rocker Step	30 seconds
Bend and Twist	45 seconds
Swing-Step Forward	30 seconds
Side Flex	45 seconds
Free Jumping	30 seconds
Sit and Stretch	45 seconds

See text, p. 194 for description of Continuity Drills.

Students alternate jump rope activity with exercises done in two-count fashion. Exercises are done with the teacher saying "Ready;" the class answers "One-two" and performs a repetition of exercise. In activities like Push-Ups and Curl-Ups, allow students to pick any challenge activity they feel capable of performing. Teachers or students can lead.

Allow students to adjust the workload to their level. This implies resting if the rope jumping is too strenuous.

See text, p. 174-186 for descriptions of exercises.

Lesson Focus – Stunts and Tumbling Skills (1)

Animal Movements

Cricket Walk

Squat. Spread the knees. Put the arms between the knees and grasp the outside of the ankles with the hands. Walk forward or backward. Chirp like a cricket. Turn around right and left. See what happens when both feet are moved at once!

Frog Jump

From a squatting position, with hands on the floor slightly in front of the feet, jump forward a short distance, landing on the hands and feet simultaneously. Note the difference between this stunt and the Rabbit Jump. Emphasis eventually should be on both height and distance. The hands and arms absorb part of the landing impact to prevent excessive strain on the knees.

Seal Crawl

Start in the front-leaning rest position, the weight supported on straightened arms and toes. Keeping the body straight, walk forward, using the hands for propelling force and dragging the feet. Keep the body straight and the head up.

Reverse Seal Crawl

Do the Seal Crawl with the tummy facing up and dragging the heels.

Six groups of activities in this lesson ensure that youngsters receive a variety of experiences. Pick a few activities from each group and teach them alternately. For example, teach one or two animal movements, then a tumbling and inverted balance, followed by a balance stunt, etc. Give equal time to each group of activities

Scatter tumbling mats throughout the area so that there is little standing in line waiting for a turn. No more than 3-4 students per mat.

Youngsters can do the animal walks around their mats. Many of the activities in this unit do not have to be performed on the mat.

Tumbling and Inverted Balances

Review the Forward Roll (taught in grades K-2)

Stand facing forward, with the feet apart. Squat and place the hands on the mat, shoulder width apart, with elbows against the insides of the thighs. Tuck the chin to the chest and make a rounded back. A push-off with the hands and feet provides the force for the roll. Carry the weight on the hands, with the elbows bearing the weight of the thighs. If the elbows are kept against the thighs and the weight is assumed there, the force of the roll is transferred easily to the rounded back. Try to roll forward to the feet. Later, try with the knees together and no weight on the elbows.

Forward Roll to a Walkout

Perform the Forward Roll as described previously, except walk out to a standing position. The key to the Walkout is to develop enough momentum to allow a return to the feet. The leg that first absorbs the weight is bent while the other leg is kept straight.

Review the Backward Curl (taught in grades K-2)

Approach this activity in three stages. For the first stage, begin in a sitting position, with the knees drawn up to the chest and the chin tucked. The hands are clasped and placed behind the head with the elbows held out as far as possible. Gently roll backward until the weight is on the elbows. Roll back to starting position.

In stage two, perform the same action as before, but place the hands alongside the head on the mat while rolling back. The fingers are pointed in the direction of the roll, with palms down on the mat. (A good cue is, "Point your thumbs toward your ears and keep your elbows close to your body.")

For stage three, perform the same action as in stage two, but start in a crouched position on the feet with the back facing the direction of the roll. Momentum is secured by sitting down quickly and bringing the knees to the chest.

Backward Roll (Handclasp Position)

Clasp the fingers behind the neck, with elbows held out to the sides. From a crouched position, sit down rapidly, bringing the knees to the chest for a tuck to secure momentum. Roll completely over backward, taking much of the weight on the forearms. With this method, the neck is protected.

Climb-Up (taught in grades K-2)

Begin on a mat in a kneeling position, with hands placed about shoulder width apart and the fingers spread and pointed forward. Place the head forward of the hands, so that the head and hands form a triangle on the mat. Walk the body weight forward so that most of it rests on the hands and head. Climb the knees to the top of the elbows. (This stunt is a lead-up to the Headstand.)

Balance Stunts

One-Leg Balance Reverse

Assume a forward balance position by balancing on one leg, bending over at the waist until the chest is parallel with the floor, and extending the arms. In a quick movement, to give momentum, swing the free leg down and change to the same forward balance position facing in the opposite direction (a 180-degree turn). No unnecessary movement of the supporting foot should be made after the turn is completed. The swinging foot should not touch the floor.

Tummy Balance

Lie prone on the floor with arms outstretched forward or to the sides, with palms down. Raise the arms, head, chest, and legs from the floor and balance on the tummy. The knees should be kept straight.

A major concern for safety is the neck and back region. Overweight children are at greater risk and might be allowed to avoid tumbling and inverted balances.

Do not perform many repetitions of tumbling and inverted balances. For most children, limiting the number of forward or backward roll repetitions to four or five will prevent fatigue and injury. The Backward Curl should be used to learn to roll back and forth. No youngster should be expected to roll over if it is difficult for them. In stunts and tumbling, it is important that the student decide if they are capable and confident enough to try the activity.

The Backward Curl is a lead-up to the Backward Roll. Teach children to push against the floor to take pressure off the back of the neck.

The handclasp position backward roll should be learned before the traditional backward roll. The handclasp method, in contrast to the traditional backward roll, does not require adequate arm strength to lift the body off the floor and release the head.

The Climb-Up should only be performed by youngsters who have sufficient strength to support the body weight. Overweight children will find this to be a difficult activity.

With the exception of the tumbling and inverted balances group, all the activities in this unit can be performed by all youngsters. If in doubt about an activity in the tumbling and inverted balances group, avoid teaching it.

This activity is excellent for back strength. It also reinforces students who are flexible in the back area.

Leg Dip

Extend both hands and one leg forward, balancing on the other leg. Lower the body to sit on the heel and return without losing the balance or touching the floor with any part of the body. Try with the other foot.

When doing the Leg Dip, another student can assist from the back by applying upward pressure to the elbows.

Individual Stunts

Reach-Under

Take a position with the feet pointed ahead (spaced about 2 feet apart) and toes against a line or a floor board. Place a beanbag two boards in front of, and midway between, the feet. Without changing the position of the feet, reach one hand behind and between the legs to pick up the beanbag. Now pick up with the other hand. Repeat, moving the beanbag a board farther away each time.

If a beanbag is unavailable, youngsters can see how far they can gradually reach and note the distance in relationship to a tile, piece of grass, or board in the floor.

Stiff Person Bend

Place the feet about shoulder width apart and pointed forward. Place a beanbag a few inches behind the right heel. Grasp the left toes with the left hand, thumb on top. Without bending the knees, reach the right hand outside the right leg and pick up the beanbag without releasing the hold on the left toes

These are enjoyable challenges for youngsters. Increase the challenge by gradually increasing the distance of the reach. Reverse sides of the body.

Coffee Grinder

Put one hand on the floor and extend the body to the floor on that side in a side-leaning rest position. Walk around the hand, making a complete circle and keeping the body straight.

The Coffee Grinder should be done slowly, with controlled movements. The body should remain as straight as possible throughout the circle movement.

Scooter

Sit on the floor with legs extended, arms folded in front of the chest, and chin held high. To scoot, pull the seat toward the heels, using heel pressure and lifting the seat slightly. Extend the legs forward again and repeat the process.

Partner and Group Stunts

Find a partner who is similar in ability.

Partner Hopping

Partners coordinate hopping movements for short distances and in different directions and turns. Three combinations are suggested.
1. Stand facing each other. Extend the right leg forward to be grasped at the ankle by partner's left hand. Hold right hands and hop on the left leg.
2. Stand back to back. Lift the leg backward, bending the knee, and have partner grasp the ankle. Hop as before.
3. Stand side by side with inside arms around each other's waist. Lift the inside foot from the floor and make progress by hopping on the outside foot.

If either partner begins to fall, the other should release the leg immediately. Reverse foot positions.

Partner Twister

Partners face and grasp right hands as if shaking hands. One partner swings the left leg over the head of the other and turns around, taking a straddle position over partner's arm. The other swings the right leg over the first partner, who has bent over, and the partners are now back to back. First partner continues with the right leg and faces in the original direction. Second partner swings the left leg over the partner's back to return to the original face-to-face position.

Partners need to duck to avoid being kicked by each other's feet as the legs are swung over.

Partner Pull-Up

Partners sit facing each other in a bent-knee position, with heels on the floor and toes touching. Pulling cooperatively, they come to a standing position.

The goal is to *simultaneously* come to the standing position, instead of one standing and pulling the other to their feet.

Game Activity

Whistle Mixer

Supplies: A whistle
Skills: All basic locomotor movements

Children are scattered throughout the area. To begin, they walk around in any direction they wish. The teacher blows a whistle a number of times in succession with short, sharp blasts. Children then form small circles with the number in the circles equal to the number of whistle blasts. If there are four blasts, children form circles of four--no more, no less. The goal is not to be left out or caught in a circle with the incorrect number of students. Children should be encouraged to move to the center of the area and raise their hands to facilitate finding others without a group. After the circles are formed, the teacher calls "Walk," and the game continues. In walking, children should move in different directions.

Variation: A fine version of this game is done with the aid of a tom-tom. Different beats indicate different locomotor movements--skipping, galloping, slow walking, normal walking, running. The whistle is still used to set the number for each circle.

Circle Contests

Supplies: Volleyballs or 8-in. foam rubber balls, two bowling pins

Skills: Throwing, catching

Two teams arranged in independent circles compete against each other. The circles should be of the same size; lines can be drawn on the floor to ensure this. The players of each team are numbered consecutively so that each player in one circle corresponds to a player in the other circle. The numbered players, in sequence, go to the center of the opponents' circle to compete for their team in either of the following activities.

1. Circle Club Guard. The center player guards a bowling pin. The circle that knocks down the club first wins a point. The ball should be rolled at the club.

2. Touch Ball. The circle players pass the ball from one to another while the center player tries to touch it. The center player who touches the ball first wins a point for the respective team. In case neither player is able to touch the ball in a reasonable period of time, the action should be cut off without awarding a point.

After all players have competed, the team with the most points wins. For Circle Club Guard, there must be three passes to different people before the ball can be thrown at the center. Establishing circle lines may be necessary to regulate throwing distance.

Alaska Baseball

Supplies: A volleyball or soccer ball

Skills: Kicking, batting, running, ball handling

The players are organized in two teams, one of which is at bat while the other is in the field. A straight line provides the only out-of-bounds line, and the team at bat is behind this line at about the middle. The other team is scattered around the fair territory.

One player propels the ball, either batting a volleyball or kicking a stationary soccer ball. His teammates are in a close file behind him. As soon as the batter sends the ball into the playing area, he starts to run around his own team. Each time the runner passes the head of the file, the team gives a loud count.

There are no outs. The first fielder to get the ball stands still and starts to pass the ball back overhead to the nearest teammate, who moves directly behind to receive it. The remainder of the team in the field must run to the ball and form a file behind it. The ball is passed back overhead, with each player handling the ball. When the last field player in line has a firm grip on it, she shouts "Stop." At this signal, a count is made of the number of times the batter ran around his own team. To score more sharply, half rounds should be counted.

Five batters or half of the team should bat; then the teams should change places. This is better than allowing an entire team to bat before changing to the field, because players in the field tire from many consecutive runs.

Variation: Regular bases can be set up, and the batter can run the bases. Scoring can be in terms of a home run made or not; or the batter can continue around the bases, getting a point for each base.

Lesson Plans for Grades 3-4 - Week 16
Rhythmic Movement (2)

Objectives:
To imitate movements of other students
To perform a variety of locomotor movements in a rhythmic setting
To understand the difference between compliance and non-compliance of game rules

Equipment Required:
One jump rope for each student
Music for exercises and rhythmic activities
Bowling pins and balls for game

Instructional Activities		Teaching Hints

Introductory Activity -- Following Activity

One partner leads and performs combinations of locomotor and non-locomotor movements. The other partner follows and performs the same movements. This can also be used with groups of 3-4 students following a leader.

Change the leaders often so all students get a chance to create some movements.

Fitness Development Activity -- Continuity Drills

Rope Jumping - Forward	30 seconds	Students alternate jump rope activity with exercises done in two-count fashion. Exercises are done with the teacher saying "Ready;" the class answers "One-two" and performs a repetition of exercise. In activities like Push-Ups and Curl-Ups, allow students to pick any challenge activity they feel capable of performing. See text, p. 163-167 for descriptions of challenges.
Double Crab Kick	45 seconds	
Rope Jumping - Backward	30 seconds	
Knee Touch Curl-Up	45 seconds	
Jump and Slowly Turn Body	30 seconds	
Push-Up Challenges	45 seconds	
Rocker Step	30 seconds	
Bend and Twist	45 seconds	
Swing-Step Forward	30 seconds	
Side Flex	45 seconds	
Free Jumping	30 seconds	
Sit and Stretch	45 seconds	Allow students to adjust the workload to their level. This implies resting if the rope jumping is too strenuous.

See text, p. 194 for description of Continuity Drills.

Lesson Focus -- Rhythmic Movement (2)

Begin each lesson with a review of one or two dances youngsters know and enjoy. Review dances from lesson plan #11 as desired before teaching new ones.

Rhythms should be taught like other sport skills. Avoid striving for perfection so students know it is acceptable to make mistakes. Teach a variety of dances rather than one or two in depth in case some students find it difficult to master a specific dance. Make dances easy for students to learn by implementing some of the following techniques:

1. Teach the dances without using partners.
2. Allow youngsters to move in any direction without left-right orientation.
3. Use scattered formation instead of circles.
4. Emphasize strong movements such as clapping and stamping to increase involvement.
5. Play the music at a slower speed when first learning the dance.

When introducing a dance, use the following methodology:
1. Tell about the dance and listen to the music.
2. Clap the beat and learn the verse.
3. Practice the dance steps without the music and with verbal cues.
4. Practice the dance with the music.

Records can be ordered from Wagon Wheel Records, 17191 Corbina Lane #203, Huntington Beach, CA (714) 846-8169.

Wild Turkey Mixer

Record: GR 15008
Formation: Trios abreast facing counterclockwise around the circle
Directions:
Measures Action
1--8   In lines of three, with the right and left person holding the near hand of the center person, all walk 16 steps forward. (Walk, 2, 3, . . . 16)
9--12   The center person (Wild Turkey) turns the right-hand person once around with the right elbow. (Turn, 2, 3, 4, 5, 6, 7, 8)

13--16 The Wild Turkey turns the left-hand person with the left elbow, and then moves forward to repeat the dance with the two new people ahead. (Turn, 2, 3, 4; Forward, 2, 3, 4)

This dance can be adapted to other pieces of music. With a faster tempo, the elbow swings are done with a skip instead of a walk.

Patty Cake (Heel and Toe) Polka (International)

Records: MAC 5003; LS E-24; Windsor 4624

Formation: Double circle, partners facing, A in the inner circle with back to the center. Both hands are joined with partner. A's left and B's right foot are free.

Directions:

Measures	Part I Action
1--2	Heel-toe twice with A's left and B's right foot. (Heel, toe, heel, toe)
3--4	Take four slides sideward to A's left, progressing counterclockwise. Do not transfer the weight on the last count. Finish with A's right and B's left foot free. (Slide, 2, 3, 4)
5--8	Repeat the pattern of measures 1--4, starting with A's right and B's left foot, progressing clockwise. Finish with the partners separated and facing. (Heel, toe, heel, toe; slide, 2, 3, 4)

Measures	Part II Action
9	Clap right hands with partner three times. (Right, 2, 3)
10	Clap left hands with partner three times. (Left, 2, 3)
11	Clap both hands with partner three times. (Both, 2, 3)
12	Slap own knees three times. (Knees, 2, 3)
13--14	Right elbow swing with partner. Partners hook right elbows and swing once around with four walking steps, finishing with A's back to center. (Swing, 2, 3, 4)
15--16	Progress left to a new partner with four walking steps. (Left, 2, 3, 4)

Repeat the entire dance with the new partner.

Oh, Susanna (American)

Records: LS E-14, E-23; MAV 1043; RPT 317

Formation: Single circle, all facing center, partner B on the right

Directions:

Measures	Part I Action
1--4	Partners B walk forward four steps and back four, as partners A clap hands. (Forward, 2, 3, 4; Back, 2, 3, 4)
5--8	Reverse, with As walking forward and back, and Bs clapping time. (Forward, 2, 3, 4; Back, 2, 3, 4)

Measures	Part II Action
1--8	Partners face each other, and all do a grand right and left by grasping the partner's right hand, then passing to the next person with a left-hand hold. Continue until reaching the seventh person, who becomes the new partner. (Face, 2, 3, 4, 5, 6, 7, 8)

Measures	Chorus
1--16	All join hands in promenade position with the new partner and walk counterclockwise around the circle for two full choruses (Promenade, 2, 3, . . . 16)

Repeat the dance from the beginning, each time with a new partner. For variety in the chorus, skip instead of walk, or walk during the first chorus and swing one's partner in place during the second chorus.

Troika (Russian)

Records: WT 10010; CM 1160

Formation: Trios face counterclockwise. Start with hands joined in a line of three. The body weight is on the left foot; the right foot is free.

Directions:

Measures	Part I Action
1	Take four running steps diagonally forward right, starting with the right foot. (Diagonal, 2, 3, 4)
2	Take four running steps diagonally forward left, starting with the right foot. (Diagonal, 2, 3, 4)
3--4	Take eight running steps in a forward direction, starting with the right foot. (Forward, 2, 3, 4, 5, 6, 7, 8)
5--6	The center dancer and the left-hand partner raise joined hands to form an arch and run in place. Meanwhile, the right-hand partner moves counterclockwise around the center dancer with eight running steps, goes under the arch, and back to place. The center dancer unwinds by turning under the arch. (Under, 2, 3, 4; Turn, 2, 3, 4)
7--8	Repeat the pattern of measures 5 and 6, with the left-hand partner running under the arch formed by the center dancer and the right-hand partner. (Under, 2, 3, 4; Turn, 2, 3, circle)

Measures	**Part II Action**
9--11	The trio joins hands and circles left with 12 running steps. (Run, 2, 3, 4, 5, 6, 7, 8, 9, 10, 11, 12)
12	Three stamps in place (counts 1--3), pause (count 4). (Stamp, 2, 3, pause)
13--15	The trio circles right with 12 running steps, opening out at the end to re-form in lines of three facing counterclockwise. (Run, 2, 3, 4, 5, 6, 7, 8, open, 10, 11, 12)
16	The center dancer releases each partner's hand and runs under the opposite arch of joined hands to advance to a new pair ahead.

Right- and left-hand partners run in place while waiting for a new center dancer to join them in a new trio. (Stamp, 2, line, pause)

Game Activity

Fox Hunt

Supplies: None

Skills: Running, dodging

Two players form trees by facing each other and holding hands. The third member of the group is a fox and stands between the hands of the trees. Three players are identified as foxes without trees and three players are designated as hounds. The hounds try to tag foxes who are not in trees. The extra foxes may move to a tree and displace the fox who is standing in the tree. In addition, the foxes in trees may leave the safety of their trees at any time. If the hound tags a fox, their roles are reversed immediately, the fox becoming the hound.

The game should be stopped at regular intervals to allow the players who are trees to change places with the foxes and hounds. Different locomotor movements can be specified to add variety to the game.

Steal the Treasure

Supplies: A bowling pin

Skill: Dodging

A playing area 20 ft square is outlined, with a small circle in the center. A bowling pin placed in the circle is the treasure. A guard is set to protect the treasure. Players then enter the square and try to steal the treasure without getting caught. The guard tries to tag them. Anyone tagged must retire and wait for the next game. The player who gets the treasure is the next guard. Teaching suggestion: If getting the treasure seems too easy, the child can be required to carry the treasure to the boundary of the square without being tagged.

Addition Tag

Supplies: None

Skills: Running, dodging

Two couples are it, and each stands with inside hands joined. These are the taggers. The other children run individually. The couples move around the playground, trying to tag with the free hands. The first person tagged joins the couple, making a trio. The three then chase until they catch a fourth. Once a fourth person is caught, the four divide and form two couples, adding another set of taggers to the game. This continues until all children are tagged.

Teaching suggestions: Some limitation of area should be established to enable the couples to catch the runners; otherwise, the game moves slowly and is fatiguing. The game moves faster if started with two couples. A tag is legal only when the couple or group of three keeps their hands joined. The game can be used as an introductory activity, since all children are active.

Lesson Plans for Grades 3-4 - Week 17
Football Related Activities (1)

Objectives:
To leap over a partner without touching the obstacle
To correctly perform partner resistance exercises
To be able to throw and catch a football

Equipment Required:
Signs and music for fitness activities
One foam rubber junior football for each
  two students
Pinnies to identify teams

Instructional Activities	Teaching Hints

Introductory Activity -- Partner Leaping

Two youngsters work together. One partner leaps over the other, moves forward 5 to 10 steps, and curls on the floor. The other partner now leaps over their partner and repeats the pattern. Increase the distance students must run before assuming the curled position on the floor.

Add some locomotor movements or stunts that youngsters must perform before leaping over their partner.

Fitness Development Activity -- Aerobic Fitness and Partner Resistance Exercises

Students find a partner and lead each other in aerobic activities. Partners switch leader and follower roles after each partner resistance exercise. This routine assumes that students have previous aerobic fitness experience. If not, the aerobic activities will have to be led by the teacher.

Bounce and Clap	25 seconds
Arm Curl-Up	45 seconds
Jumping Jack variations	25 seconds
Camelback	45 seconds
Lunge variations	25 seconds
Fist Pull apart	45 seconds
Directional Runs	25 seconds
Scissors	45 seconds
Rhythmic Running	25 seconds
Butterfly	45 seconds
Bounce with Body Twist	25 seconds
Resistance Push-Up	45 seconds

Walk, stretch, and relax for a minute or two.

Tape alternating segments of silence and music to signal duration of exercise. Music segments indicate aerobic activity (25 seconds) while intervals of silence announce partner resistance exercises (45 seconds).

Teach the exercises first; See text, p. 195-199 for descriptions of aerobic activities. See text, p. 187-189 for descriptions of partner resistance exercises. A sign with aerobic activities on one side and partner resistance exercises on the other help students remember the activities. The signs can be held upright by cones and shared by 2-4 students.

Take 6-10 seconds to complete a resistance exercise.

Lesson Focus -- Football-Related Activities

Skills
Practice the following skills:
1. Forward Passing
   The ball should be gripped lightly behind the middle with the fingers on the lace. The thumbs and fingers should be relaxed. In throwing, the opposing foot should point in the direction of the pass, with the body turned sideways. In preparation for the pass, the ball is raised up and held over the shoulders. The ball is delivered directly forward with an overhand movement of the arm and with the index finger pointing toward the line of flight.
2. Catching
   When making a catch, the receiver should keep both eyes on the ball and catch it in the hands with a slight give. As soon as the ball is caught, it should be tucked into the carrying position. The little fingers are together for most catches.
3. Centering
   Centering involves transferring the ball, on a signal, to the quarterback. In elementary school, the shotgun formation is most often used. This requires snapping the ball a few yards backward to the quarterback. A direct snap involves placing the hands under the buttocks of the center. The ball is then lifted, rotated a quarter turn, and snapped into the hands of the quarterback.

Use instructional cues to improve throwing techniques:
1. Turn the nonthrowing side toward the direction of the throw.
2. Throw the ball with an overhand motion.
3. Step toward the pass receiver.

The following instructional cues will focus on catching technique:
1. Thumbs together for a high pass (above shoulder level).
2. Thumbs apart for a low pass (below shoulder level).
3. Reach for the ball, give, and bring the ball to the body.

The centering player takes a position with the feet well spread and toes pointed straight ahead. Knees are bent and close enough to the ball to reach it with a slight stretch. The right hand takes about the same grip as is used in passing. The other hand is on the side near the back of the ball and merely acts as a guide. On signal from the quarterback, the center extends the arms backward through the legs and centers the ball to the quarterback.

Drills
Set up stations for skill practice. Rotate students to each station.
Station 1 - Stance Practice
Students work with a partner and practice getting into the proper stance position. When stance form is mastered, partners can practice getting into position and racing to cones five yards away.
Station 2 - Centering to a Partner
Students work in pairs and practice centering to each other.
Station 3 - Passing and Receiving with a Partner
Students work in pairs and practice passing and receiving the ball. Place emphasis on proper throwing and catching technique.
Station 4 - Pass Defense Drill
Work in groups of three. One player is the passer, one the receiver, and one the defensive player. The passer takes the ball, calls the signal for the receiver to run a pattern, and passes to the receiver who is covered by the defensive player

Instructional cues for centering include the following:
1. Reach forward for the ball.
2. Snap the ball with the dominant hand.
3. Guide the ball with the nondominant hand.

Signs which describe key points for each skill should be placed on cones at each station. Instructional cues should also be placed on the signs so students can analyze their form and performance.

Use foam rubber footballs with third and fourth graders. This helps students learn the skills without fear of being hurt by the ball.

Game Activity

Football End Ball
Supplies: Footballs
Skills: Passing, catching
The court is divided in half by a centerline. End zones are marked 3 ft wide, completely across the court at each end. Players on each team are divided into three groups: forwards, guards, and ends. The object is for a forward to throw successfully to one of the end-zone players. End-zone players take positions in one of the end zones. Their forwards and guards then occupy the half of the court farthest from this end zone. The forwards are near the centerline, and the guards are back near the end zone of their half of the court.

The ball is put into play with a center jump between the two tallest opposing forwards. When a team gets the ball, the forwards try to throw over the heads of the opposing team to an end-zone player. To score, the ball must be caught by an end-zone player with both feet inside the zone. No moving with the ball is permitted by any player. After each score, play is resumed by a jump ball at the centerline.

A penalty results in loss of the ball to the other team. Penalties are assessed for the following.
1. Holding a ball for more than 5 seconds
2. Stepping over the end line or stepping over the centerline into the opponent's territory
3. Pushing or holding another player

In case of an out-of-bounds ball, the ball belongs to the team that did not cause it to go out. The nearest player retrieves the ball at the sideline and returns it to a player of the proper team.

Teaching suggestions: Fast, accurate passing is to be encouraged. Players in the end zones must practice jumping high to catch the ball while still landing with both feet inside the end-zone area. A system of rotation is desirable. Each time a score is made, players on that team can rotate one person.

To outline the end zones, some instructors use folding mats (4 by 7 ft or 4 by 8 ft). Three or four mats forming each end zone make a definite area and eliminate the problem of defensive players (guards) stepping into the end zone.

Five Passes
Supplies: A football, pinnies or other identification
Skills: Passing, catching
Players scatter on the field. The object of the game is for one team to make five consecutive passes to five different players without losing control of the ball. This scores 1 point. The defense may play the ball only and may not make personal contact with opposing players. No player can take more than three steps when in possession of the ball. More than three steps is called traveling, and the ball is awarded to the other team.

The ball is given to the opponents at the nearest out-of-bounds line for traveling, minor contact fouls, after a point has been scored, and for causing the ball to go out-of-bounds. No penalty is assigned when the ball hits the ground. It remains in play, but the five-pass sequence is interrupted and must start again. Jump balls are called when the ball is tied up or when there is a pileup. The official should call out the pass sequence.

Lesson Plans for Grades 3-4 - Week 18
Basketball Related Activities

Objectives:
To understand the basic rules of basketball
To dribble, pass and shoot a basketball with proper form
To participate in basketball lead-up games

Equipment Required:
One junior basketball or playground ball
    per student
Music for exercises
8 hoops or individual mats
Pinnies

Instructional Activities	Teaching Hints

Introductory Activity -- Bridges by Three

Children work in groups of three, with two of the children making bridges and the third moving under them. As soon as the third person has moved under the others, she makes a bridge. Each child in turn goes under the bridge of the other two students.

Avoid touching fellow students while moving under the bridges. Stipulate that students have to run 10 steps after going under both bridges.

Fitness Development Activity -- Aerobic Fitness and Partner Resistance Exercises

Students find a partner and lead each other in aerobic activities. Partners switch leader and follower roles after each partner resistance exercise. This routine assumes that students have previous aerobic fitness experience. If not, the aerobic activities will have to be led by the teacher.

Bounce and Clap	25 seconds
Arm Curl-Up	45 seconds
Jumping Jack Variations	25 seconds
Camelback	45 seconds
Lunge Variations	25 seconds
Fist Pull Apart	45 seconds
Directional Runs	25 seconds
Scissors	45 seconds
Rhythmic Running	25 seconds
Butterfly	45 seconds
Bounce with Body Twist	25 seconds
Resistance Push-Up	45 seconds

Walk, stretch, and relax for a minute or two.

Tape alternating segments of silence and music to signal duration of exercise. Music segments indicate aerobic activity (25 seconds) while intervals of silence announce partner resistance exercises (45 seconds).

Teach the exercises first; See text, p. 195-199 for descriptions of aerobic activities. See text, p. 187-189 for descriptions of partner resistance exercises. A sign with aerobic activities on one side and partner resistance exercises on the other help students remember the activities. The signs can be held upright by cones and shared by 2-4 students.

Take 6-10 seconds to complete a resistance exercise.

Lesson Focus -- Basketball-Related Activities (1)

Skills
Practice the following skills:
1. Chest (or Two-Hand) Pass

For the chest, or two-hand, pass, one foot is ahead of the other, with the knees flexed slightly. The ball is released at chest level, with the fingers spread on each side of the ball. The elbows remain close to the body, and the ball is released by extending the arms and snapping the wrists as one foot moves toward the receiver.
2. Catching

Receiving the ball is a most important fundamental skill. Many turnovers involve failure to handle a pass properly. The receiver should move toward the pass with the fingers spread and relaxed, reaching for the ball with elbows bent and wrists relaxed. The hands should give as the ball comes in.
3. Dribbling

Dribbling is used to advance the ball, break for a basket, or maneuver out of a difficult situation. The dribbler's knees and trunk should be slightly flexed, with hands and eyes forward. The ball is propelled by the fingertips with the hand cupped and relaxed. There is little arm motion. Younger children tend to slap at the ball rather than push it. The dribbling hand should be alternated, and practice in changing hands is essential.

Instructional cues help students focus on proper performance of passing.
1. Fingers spread with thumbs behind the ball.
2. Elbows in; extend through the ball.
3. Step forward, extend arms, and rotate hands slightly inward.
4. Throw at chest level to the receiver.
5. For bounce passes, bounce the ball past the halfway point nearer the receiver.

Instructional cues for catching include the following:
1. Move into the path of the ball.
2. Reach and give with the ball (absorb the force of the ball by reaching and bringing the ball to the chest).

4. Shooting - One-Hand (set) Push Shot

The one-hand push shot is used as a set shot for young children. The ball is held at shoulder-eye level in the supporting hand with the shooting hand slightly below center and behind the ball. As the shot begins, the supporting (non-shooting) hand remains in contact as long as possible. The shooting hand then takes over with fingertip control, and the ball rolls off the center three fingers. The hand and wrist follow through, finishing in a flexed position. Vision is focused on the hoop during the shot. Proper technique should be emphasized rather than accuracy.

Drills

Passing and Catching Drills
1. Slide Circle Drill

In the slide circle drill, a circle of four to six players slides around a person in the center. The center person passes to and receives from the sliding players. After the ball has gone around the circle twice, another player takes the center position.
2. Circle-Star Drill

With only five players, a circle-star drill is particularly effective. Players pass to every other player, and the path of the ball forms a star. The star drill works well as a relay. Any odd number of players will cause the ball to go to all participants, assuring that all receive equal practice.

Dribbling Drills
3. Random Dribbling

Each child has a ball. Dribbling is done in place, varied by using left and right hands. Develop a sequence of body positions (i.e., standing, kneeling, lying on the side, on two feet and one hand). Encourage players to develop a sequence by dribbling a certain number of times in each selected position. Dribble with each hand.
4. One-Hand Control Drill

Begin with the right hand holding the ball. Make a half circle around the right leg to the back. Bounce the ball between the legs (back to front) and catch it with the right hand and move it around the body again. After continuing for a short time, switch to the left hand.

Shooting Drills
5. Basic Shooting Drill

In one simple shooting drill, players form files of no more than four people, and take turns shooting a long and a short shot or some other prescribed series of shots.
6. Set-Shot Drill

In the set-shot drill, players are scattered around a basket in a semicircle, with a leader in charge. Players should be close enough to the basket so that they can shoot accurately. The leader passes to each in turn to take a shot. The leader chases the ball after the shot. A bit of competition can be injected by allowing a successful shooter to take one step back for the next shot, or a player can shoot until he misses.

Instructional cues for dribbling include the following:
1. Push the ball to the floor. Don't slap it.
2. Push the ball forward when moving.
3. Eyes forward and head up.

Shooting instructional cues focus on proper form:
1. Keep the shooting elbow near the body.
2. Bend the knees and use the legs.
3. Release the ball off the fingertips.

Baskets should be lowered to 8 or 9 feet, depending on the size of the youngsters.

Lowered baskets help students shoot with proper form. Shooting is not a throw. If students have to throw the ball at the basket, it is too high.

Practice the skills in an individual manner as much as possible. The best alternative is a ball for every student to shoot and dribble. Reduce taking turns as much as possible when practicing skills.

Use junior basketballs or smaller for third and fourth grade students. It is difficult for students to learn skills with regulations size balls. They are too heavy and to large in diameter for youngsters.

Game Activity

Birdie in the Cage

Supplies: A soccer ball, basketball, or volleyball

Skills: Passing, catching, intercepting

Players are in circle formation with one child in the middle. The object of the game is for the center player to try to touch the ball. The ball is passed from player to player in the circle, and the center player attempts to touch the ball on one of these passes. The player who threw the ball that was touched takes the place in the center. In case of a bad pass resulting in the ball's leaving the circle area, the player who caused the error can change to the center of the ring.

Teaching suggestions: The ball should move rapidly. Passing to a neighboring player is not allowed. If touching the ball proves difficult, a second center may join the first. Play can be limited to a specific type of pass (bounce, two-hand, push).

Variation: As few as three children can play, with two children passing the ball back and forth between them while a third tries to touch it. An excellent version of this game calls for four players, with three forming a triangle and positioning themselves about 15 ft apart.

Dribblerama

Supplies: One basketball for each player

Skills: Dribbling and protecting the ball

The playing area is a large circle or square, clearly outlined. All players dribble within the area. The game is played on two levels.

Level 1: Each player dribbles throughout the area, controlling the ball so that it does not touch another ball. If a touch occurs, both players go outside the area and dribble counterclockwise around the area. Once youngsters have completed dribbling one lap around the path, they can reenter the game.

Level 2: While dribbling and controlling the ball, each player attempts to cause another player to lose control of the ball. When control is lost, that player takes the ball and dribbles around the perimeter of the area. Play continues until only two or three players who have not lost control of their ball are left. These are declared the winners. Bring all players back into the game and repeat.

Captain Ball

Supplies: A basketball, pinnies, eight hoops or individual mats

Skills: Passing, catching, guarding

Two games can be played crosswise on a basketball court. A centerline is needed and the normal out-of-bounds lines can be used. Hoops or individual mats can provide the markers for the forwards and the captains. Captain Ball is a very popular game that is played with many variations. In this version, a team is composed of a captain, three forwards, and three guards. The guards throw the ball to their captain. The captain and the three forwards are each assigned to respective circles and must always keep one foot inside the circle. Guarding these four circle players are three guards.

The game is started by a jump at the centerline by two guards from opposing teams. The guards can rove in their half of the court but must not enter the circles of the opposing players. The ball is put into play after each score in much the same manner as in regular basketball. The team scored on puts the ball into play by a guard throwing the ball in bounds from the side of the court.

As soon as a guard gets the ball, he throws it to one of the forwards, who must maneuver to be open. The forward then tries to throw it to the other forwards or in, to the captain. Two points are scored when all three forwards handle the ball and then it is passed to the captain. One point is scored when the ball is passed to the captain but has not been handled by all three forwards.

Stepping over the centerline is a foul. It is also a foul if a guard steps into a circle or makes personal contact with a circle player. The penalty for a foul is a free throw.

For a free throw, the ball is given to an unguarded forward, who has 5 seconds to get the ball successfully to the guarded captain. If the throw is successful, one point is scored. If it is not successful, the ball is in play. Successive fouls rotate free throws among the forwards.

As in basketball, when the ball goes out-of-bounds, it is awarded to the team that did not cause it to go out. If a forward or a captain catches a ball with both feet out of her circle, the ball is taken out-of-bounds by the opposing guard. For violations such as traveling or kicking the ball, the ball is awarded to an opposing guard out-of-bounds. No score may be made from a ball that is thrown in directly from out-of-bounds.

Teaching suggestions: Some instruction is necessary for children to absorb the basic strategy of the game. An effective offensive formation is to space the guards along the centerline. Only the offensive team is diagrammed. By passing the ball back and forth among the guards, the forwards have more opportunity to be open, since the passing makes the guards shift position.

The guards may dribble, but this should be held to a minimum and used for advancing the ball only when necessary. Otherwise, dribbling accomplishes little.

The forwards and the captain should learn to shift back and forth to become open for passes. Considerable latitude is available, since they need keep only one foot in the hoop. Short and accurate passing uses both high and bounce passes. Circle players may jump for the ball but must come down with one foot in the circle.

Variations:

1. Four guards can be used, but scoring is then more difficult.

2. A five-circle formation can be used, forming a five spot like that on a die. Nine players are needed on each team: four forwards, four guards, and one captain.

3. A platform 6 to 8 in. high and 20 in. square can elevate the captain to make reception of the ball easier.

Basketball Tag

Supplies: A foam rubber basketball, pinnies

Skills: Catching, passing, dribbling, guarding

Designate three to five students to be it and wear a pinny. The rest of the class passes the ball and tries to tag one of the students who is it with the ball. If desired, more than one ball can be used. More than one ball can be used and more than one player per team can be identified as it.

Lesson Plans for Grades 3-4 - Week 19
Basketball Related Activities (2)

Objectives:
To perform fitness challenges that are physically challenging
To perform defensive skills
To shoot the lay-up shot
To participate as a team member in basketball leadup games

Equipment Required:
One jump rope for each student
One junior basketball or playground ball per student
Music for exercises
8 hoops or individual mats
Pinnies

Instructional Activities	Teaching Hints

Introductory Activity -- Jumping and Hopping Patterns

Students jump or hop to a target area and return with a different pattern. Many combinations can be devised with the basic idea being to develop a pattern to get to the target and another to return to home spot. An example is: Jump in all directions and hop back to place; or three jumps forward and a half twist, three jumps back to place and a half twist.

Encourage students to develop personal combinations of movement.

Increase the distance of movement as the patterns are developed.

Fitness Development Activity -- Fitness Challenges and Rope Jumping

Alternate rope jumping with strength and flexibility challenges. Repeat the challenges as necessary.
1. Jump rope for 45 seconds
2. Perform Flexibility and Trunk Development Challenges - 45 seconds
    1. Bend in different directions.
    2. Stretch slowly and return quickly.
    3. Combine bending and stretching movements.
    4. Sway back and forth.
    5. Twist one body part; add body parts.
    6. Make your body move in a large circle.
    7. In a sitting position, wave your legs at a friend; make circles with your legs.
3. Jump rope for 45 seconds
4. Perform Shoulder Girdle Challenges - 45 seconds
    In a push-up position, do the following challenges:
    1. Lift one foot; the other foot.
    2. Wave at a friend; wave with the other arm.
    3. Scratch your back with one hand; use the other hand.
    4. Walk your feet to your hands.
    5. Turn over and face the ceiling; shake a leg; Crab Walk.
5. Jump rope for 45 seconds
6. Perform Abdominal Development - 45 seconds
    From a supine position:
    1. Lift your head and look at your toes.
    2. Lift your knees to your chest.
    3. Wave your legs at a friend.
    From a sitting position:
    1. Slowly lay down with hands on tummy.
    2. Lift legs and touch toes.
7. Jump rope for 45 seconds

Tape alternating segments (45 seconds in length) of silence and music to signal duration of exercise. Music segments indicate doing the locomotor movements while intervals of silence announce performing the strength and flexibility challenges

See text, p. 163-167 for descriptions of challenges.

Students select the fitness challenge they feel capable of performing. This implies that not all youngsters are required to do the same workload. Children differ and their ability to perform fitness workloads differs. Make fitness a personal challenge.

See the rope jumping lesson plan (p. 29-30) for different rope jumping step variations. Encourage students to practice a slow and fast time rhythms.

Lesson Focus -- Basketball-Related Activities (2)

Skills:
Review skills from the previous lesson plan which include passing, catching, dribbling, set shot. Introduce new skills:
1. Defending
    Defending involves bending the knees slightly, spreading the feet, and facing the opponent at a distance of about 3 feet. The weight should be distributed evenly on both feet to allow for movement in any direction. Sideward movement is done with a sliding motion. The defender should wave one hand to distract the opponent and to block passes and shots.

Instructional cues for proper defending are as follows:

1. Keep the knees bent.
2. Keep the hands up.
3. Don't cross the feet when moving.

2. Lay-Up Shot

The lay-up is a short shot taken when going in toward the basket either after receiving a pass or at the end of a dribble. In a shot from the right side, the takeoff is with the left foot, and vice versa. The ball is carried with both hands early in the shot and then shifted to one hand for the final push. The ball, guided by the fingertips, should be laid against the backboard with a minimum of spin.

Drills:

Review previous drills learned in the previous lesson and introduce the following:

1. Group Defensive Drill

For the group defensive drill, the entire class is scattered on a basketball floor, facing one of the sides. The instructor or the student leader stands on the side, near the center. The leader points in one direction (forward, backward, or to one side) and gives the command "Move." When the students have moved a short distance, the leader commands, "Stop." Players keep good defensive position throughout.

2. Lay-Up Drill

Two short lines of players are placed; one to the left of the basket and the other on the right side of the basket. One line passes to the other line for lay-up shots. Shooters come in from the right side first (this is easier), then from the left, and finally from the center. Each player goes to the end of the other line.

Instructional cues for the lay-up shot are:
1. Take off on the foot opposite the shooting hand

2. Lay the ball on the backboard above the basketball.
3. Jump upward and slightly forward on the takeoff.

Commands can be changed so that movement is continuous. Commands are "Right," "Left," "Forward," "Backward," and "Stop." The leader must watch that movement is not so far in any one direction that it causes players to run into obstructions. Commands can be given in order, and pointing can accompany commands.

Game Activity

Captain Ball

Supplies: A basketball, pinnies, eight hoops or individual mats

Skills: Passing, catching, guarding

Two games can be played crosswise on a basketball court. A centerline is needed and the normal out-of-bounds lines can be used. Hoops or individual mats can provide the markers for the forwards and the captains. Captain Ball is a very popular game that is played with many variations. In this version, a team is composed of a captain, three forwards, and three guards. The guards throw the ball to their captain. The captain and the three forwards are each assigned to respective circles and must always keep one foot inside the circle. Guarding these four circle players are three guards.

The game is started by a jump at the centerline by two guards from opposing teams. The guards can rove in their half of the court but must not enter the circles of the opposing players. The ball is put into play after each score in much the same manner as in regular basketball. The team scored on puts the ball into play by a guard throwing the ball in bounds from the side of the court.

As soon as a guard gets the ball, he throws it to one of the forwards, who must maneuver to be open. The forward then tries to throw it to the other forwards or in, to the captain. Two points are scored when all three forwards handle the ball and then it is passed to the captain. One point is scored when the ball is passed to the captain but has not been handled by all three forwards.

Stepping over the centerline is a foul. It is also a foul if a guard steps into a circle or makes personal contact with a circle player. The penalty for a foul is a free throw.

For a free throw, the ball is given to an unguarded forward, who has 5 seconds to get the ball successfully to the guarded captain. If the throw is successful, one point is scored. If it is not successful, the ball is in play. Successive fouls rotate free throws among the forwards.

As in basketball, when the ball goes out-of-bounds, it is awarded to the team that did not cause it to go out. If a forward or a captain catches a ball with both feet out of her circle, the ball is taken out-of-bounds by the opposing guard. For violations such as traveling or kicking the ball, the ball is awarded to an opposing guard out-of-bounds. No score may be made from a ball that is thrown in directly from out-of-bounds.

Teaching suggestions: Some instruction is necessary for children to absorb the basic strategy of the game. An effective offensive formation is to space the guards along the centerline. Only the offensive team is diagrammed. By passing the ball back and forth among the guards, the forwards have more opportunity to be open, since the passing makes the guards shift position.

The guards may dribble, but this should be held to a minimum and used for advancing the ball only when necessary. Otherwise, dribbling accomplishes little.

The forwards and the captain should learn to shift back and forth to become open for passes. Considerable latitude is available, since they need keep only one foot in the hoop. Short and accurate passing uses both high and bounce passes. Circle players may jump for the ball but must come down with one foot in the circle.

Five Passes

    Supplies: A basketball; colored shirts, markers, or pinnies

    Skills: Passing, guarding

    Two teams play. The object of the game is to complete five consecutive passes, which scores a point. On one basketball floor, two games can proceed at the same time, one in each half.

    The game is started with a jump ball at the free-throw line. The teams observe regular basketball rules in ball handling and with regard to traveling and fouling. Five consecutive passes must be made by a team, who count out loud as the passes are completed.

    The ball must not be passed back to the person from whom it was received. No dribbling is allowed. If for any reason the ball is fumbled and recovered or improperly passed, a new count is started. After a successful score, the ball can be thrown up again in a center jump at the free-throw line. A foul draws a free throw, which can score a point. Teams should be well marked to avoid confusion.

Around the Key

    Supplies: A basketball

    Skill: Shooting

    Spots are arranged for shooting around the key. A player begins at the first spot and continues until a miss. When a miss occurs, the player can stop and wait for her next opportunity and begin from the point where the miss occurred, or she can "risk it" and try another shot immediately from the point where the first try was missed. If the shot is made, the player continues. If the shot is missed, the player must start over on the next turn. The winner is the player who completes the key first or who makes the most progress.

Lesson Plans for Grades 3-4 - Week 20
Recreational Activities

Objectives:
To be able to move continuously in moderately active activities
To learn the rules of recreational activities
To play in recreational activities independently without adult supervision

Equipment Required:
One yarnball for each student
One jump rope for each student
Equipment for recreational activities

Instructional Activities	Teaching Hints
Introductory Activity -- Yarnball Fun	
Each child has a yarnball. Allow students to kick, throw or move with the ball for a designated time. On signal, place the balls on the floor and perform movements around, between and over the balls.	Place the yarnballs around the perimeter of the area. When students enter, they can move to a yarnball and begin handling it.

Fitness Development Activity -- Fitness Challenges and Rope Jumping	
Alternate rope jumping with strength and flexibility challenges. Repeat the challenges as necessary.	Tape alternating segments (45 seconds in length) of silence and music to signal duration of exercise. Music segments indicate doing the locomotor movements while intervals of silence announce performing the strength and flexibility challenges
1. Jump rope for 45 seconds	
2. Perform Flexibility and Trunk Development Challenges - 45 seconds	
1. Bend in different directions.	
2. Stretch slowly and return quickly.	
3. Combine bending and stretching movements.	
4. Sway back and forth.	
5. Twist one body part; add body parts.	
6. Make your body move in a large circle.	
7. In a sitting position, wave your legs at a friend; make circles with your legs.	
3. Jump rope for 45 seconds	Students select the fitness challenge they feel capable of performing. This implies that not all youngsters are required to do the same workload. Children differ and their ability to perform fitness workloads differs. Make fitness a personal challenge.
4. Perform Shoulder Girdle Challenges - 45 seconds	
In a push-up position, do the following challenges:	
1. Lift one foot; the other foot.	
2. Wave at a friend; wave with the other arm.	
3. Scratch your back with one hand; use the other hand.	
4. Walk your feet to your hands.	
5. Turn over and face the ceiling; shake a leg; Crab Walk.	
5. Jump rope for 45 seconds	
6. Perform Abdominal Development - 45 seconds	See text, p. 163-167 for descriptions of challenges.
From a supine position:	
1. Lift your head and look at your toes.	
2. Lift your knees to your chest.	
3. Wave your legs at a friend.	See the rope jumping lesson plan (p. 29-30) for different rope jumping step variations. Encourage students to practice a slow and fast time rhythms.
From a sitting position:	
1. Slowly lay down with hands on tummy.	
2. Lift legs and touch toes.	
7. Jump rope for 45 seconds	

Lesson Focus and Game Activity -- Recreational Activities	
The purpose of this unit is to teach students activities that they can use for recreation outside of school or during recess. Suggested activities are:	Teach students the rules of recreational activities so they are able to participate effectively during free-time.
1. Shuffleboard	
2. Two Square or Four Square	
3. Hopscotch	
4. Beanbag Horseshoes	Teach any games that are traditional to an area. Older youngsters may be a good source of advice for often-played games.
5. Jacks	
6. Marbles	
7. Sidewalk tennis	
8. Quoits	If desired, set up a number of stations and have youngsters rotate to different stations during the lesson.
9. Rubber Horseshoes	
10. Any traditional and/or local area games	

Lesson Plans for Grades 3-4 - Week 21
Fundamental Skills Using Balance Beams

Objectives:
To select fitness challenges that are physically challenging
To maintain balance while doing a variety of beam challenges
To demonstrate controlled balance while manipulating equipment

Equipment Required:
6-2"X4" boards, 10 feet long
One beanbag for each student
Desired equipment for balance beam
   challenges

Instructional Activities	Teaching Hints

Introductory Activity -- Move and Manipulate

Each student has a beanbag. While moving, students toss and catch their beanbag. On freeze, they stop and play catch with a partner (using one or two beanbags)	Encourage control of the beanbag rather than high and wild tosses.

Fitness Development Activity -- Fitness Challenges and Rope Jumping

Alternate rope jumping with strength and flexibility challenges. Repeat the challenges as necessary.	Tape alternating segments (45 seconds in length) of silence and music to signal duration of exercise. Music segments indicate doing the locomotor movements while intervals of silence announce performing the strength and flexibility challenges
1. Jump rope for 45 seconds	
2. Perform Flexibility and Trunk Development Challenges - 45 seconds	
1. Bend in different directions.	
2. Stretch slowly and return quickly.	
3. Combine bending and stretching movements.	
4. Sway back and forth.	
5. Twist one body part; add body parts.	
6. Make your body move in a large circle.	See text, p. 163-167 for descriptions of challenges.
7. In a sitting position, wave your legs at a friend; make circles with your legs.	
3. Jump rope for 45 seconds	
4. Perform Shoulder Girdle Challenges - 45 seconds	
In a push-up position, do the following challenges:	Students select the fitness challenge they feel capable of performing. This implies that not all youngsters are required to do the same workload. Children differ and their ability to perform fitness workloads differs. Make fitness a personal challenge.
1. Lift one foot; the other foot.	
2. Wave at a friend; wave with the other arm.	
3. Scratch your back with one hand; use the other hand.	
4. Walk your feet to your hands.	
5. Turn over and face the ceiling; shake a leg; Crab Walk.	
5. Jump rope for 45 seconds	
6. Perform Abdominal Development - 45 seconds	
From a supine position:	
1. Lift your head and look at your toes.	
2. Lift your knees to your chest.	
3. Wave your legs at a friend.	See the rope jumping lesson plan (p. 29-30) for different rope jumping step variations. Encourage students to practice a slow and fast time rhythms.
From a sitting position:	
1. Slowly lay down with hands on tummy.	
2. Lift legs and touch toes.	
7. Jump rope for 45 seconds	

Lesson Focus -- Fundamental Skills Using Balance Beams

1. Walk length of beam.	If balance beams are not available, use 2" x 4" boards placed on the floor. This will give students some elevation off the floor and offer balance challenges.
a. Walk forward.	
b. Walk backward.	
c. Walk sideways--lead with both left and right sides of body.	
2. Walk different directions and vary arm and body positions.	
a. Hands on hips.	Place the beams parallel to each other and have a similar number of students lined up behind each one. Students progress down the beam.
b. Hands on head.	
c. Hands folded across chest.	
d. Lean to one side or the other.	
e. Body bent forward or backward.	
f. Hands on knees or feet.	
g. Exploratory activity.	

3. Balance objects such as beanbags, erasers or wands while walking across beam.
4. Move across the beam in various directions using the following movements:
   a. Slide
   b. Heel and toe
   c. Tiptoes
   d. Grapevine
   e. Dip step
5. Perform animal movements across the balance beam.
   a. Puppy dog walk
   b. Bear Walk
   c. Crab Walk
6. Use manipulative equipment while walking the beam.
   a. Play catch with beanbags. Try different throws and movements.
   b. Bounce a playground ball and catch it, dribble it, play catch with a partner.
   c. Step over a wand, go under a wand, change directions.
   d. Go through a hoop.

After moving the length of the beam, have students do a locomotor movement to the end of the teaching area and return. This will offer students both balance activities and the chance to practice locomotor movements. It also keeps students engaged in activity for a longer period of time and reduces standing and waiting time. Specified movements can be placed on return activity signs.

If a student steps off the beam, have them get back on and progress. Sometimes, students stop walking the beam and receive little practice.

Move with controlled, deliberate movements across the beam. Speed is not a goal.

Game Activity

Fly Trap

Supplies: None

Skills: Fundamental locomotor movements

Half of the class is scattered around the playing area, sitting on the floor in cross-legged fashion. These children form the trap. The other children are the flies, and they buzz around the seated children. When a whistle is blown, the flies must freeze where they are. If any of the trappers can touch a fly, that fly sits down at that spot and becomes a trapper. The trappers must keep their seats glued to the floor.

The game continues until all of the flies are caught. Some realism is given to the game if the flies make buzzing sounds and move their arms as wings.

Teaching suggestion: Some experience with the game enables the teacher to determine how far apart to place the seated children. After all (or most) of the flies have been caught, the groups trade places. The method of locomotion should be changed occasionally also.

Nonda's Car Lot

Supplies: None

Skills: Running, dodging

One player is it and stands in the center of the area between two lines established about 50 ft apart. The class selects four brands of cars (e.g., Honda, Corvette, Toyota, Cadillac). Each student then selects a car from the four but does not tell anyone what it is.

The tagger calls out a car name. All students who selected that name attempt to run to the other line without getting tagged. The tagger calls out the cars until all students have run. When a child (car) gets tagged, she must sit down at the spot of the tag. She cannot move but may tag other students who run too near her. When the one who is it calls out "Car lot," all of the cars must go. The game is played until all students have been tagged.

Lesson Plans for Grades 3-4 - Week 22
Stunts and Tumbling Skills (2)

Objectives:
To hear and move to different rhythms
To support and control body weight in a variety of stunts and tumbling activities
To participate in game activities in a cooperative manner

Equipment Required:
Tape for moving to music
Music for aerobic fitness
Tumbling mats

Instructional Activities	Teaching Hints

Introductory Activity -- Moving to Music

Use a different music to stimulate various locomotor and non-locomotor movements. Different dance steps such as polka, two-step and schottische could be practiced.

The primary purpose of this activity is to help students sense different rhythms and move to the rhythm.

Fitness Development Activity -- Aerobic Fitness

1. Rhythmic run with clap
2. Bounce turn and clap
3. Rhythmic 4-count curl-ups (knees, toes, knees, back)
4. Rhythmic Crab Kicks (slow time)
5. Jumping Jack combination
6. Double knee lifts
7. Lunges (right, left, forward) with single-arm circles (on the side lunges) and double-arms circles (on the forward lunge)
8. Rhythmic trunk twists
9. Directional run (forward, backward, side, turning)
10. Rock side to side with clap
11. Side leg raises (alternate legs)
12. Rhythmic 4-count push-ups (If these are too difficult for students, substitute single-arm circles in the push-up position.)

See text, p. 195-199 for descriptions of aerobic activities.

Use music to stimulate effort. Any combination of movements can be used.

Keep the steps simple and easy to perform. Some students will become frustrated if the learning curve is steep.

Signs which explain the aerobic activities will help students remember performance cues.

Don't stress or expect perfection. Allow students to perform the activities as best they can.

Alternate bouncing and running movements with flexibility and strength development movements.

Lesson Focus – Stunts and Tumbling Skills (2)

Animal Movements
Measuring Worm
    From a front-leaning rest position, keeping the knees stiff, inch the feet up as close as possible to the hands. Regain position by inching forward with the hands. Keep the knees straight, with the necessary bending occurring at the hips.

Mule Kick
    Stoop down and place the hands on the floor in front of the feet. The arms are the front legs of the mule. Kick out with the legs while the weight is supported momentarily on the arms. Taking the weight on the hands is important. The stunt can be learned in two stages. First, practice taking the weight momentarily on the hands. Next, add the kick.

Walrus Walk
    Begin in a front-leaning rest position, with fingers pointed outward. Make progress by moving both hands forward at the same time. Try to clap the hands with each step.

Tumbling and Inverted Balances
Frog Handstand (Tip-Up)
    Squat down on the mat, placing the hands flat, with fingers pointing forward and elbows inside and pressed against the inner part of the knees. Lean forward, using the leverage of the elbows against the knees, and balance on the hands. Hold for 5 seconds. Return to position. The head does not touch the mat at any time.

Six groups of activities in this lesson ensure that youngsters receive a variety of experiences. Pick a few activities from each group and teach them alternately. For example, teach one or two animal movements, then a tumbling and inverted balance, followed by a balance stunt, etc. Give equal time to each group of activities

Scatter tumbling mats throughout the area so that there is little standing in line waiting for a turn.

Youngsters can do the animal walks around their mats. Many of the activities in this unit do not have to be performed on the mat.

A major concern for safety is the neck and back region. Overweight children are at greater risk and might be allowed to avoid tumbling and inverted balances.

Half Teeter-Totter

This is continued lead-up activity for the Handstand. Begin in the lunge position and shift the weight to the hands. Kick the legs up in the air to a 135-degree angle, then return to the feet. This activity is similar to the Switcheroo, except that the feet are kicked higher without switching foot position.

Cartwheel

Start with the body in an erect position, arms outspread and legs shoulder width apart. Bend the body to the right and place the right hand on the floor. Follow this, in sequence, by the left hand, the left foot, and the right foot. Perform with a steady rhythm. Each body part should touch the floor at evenly spaced intervals. The body should be straight and extended when in the inverted position. The entire body must be in the same plane throughout the stunt, and the feet must pass directly overhead.

Balance Stunts
Leg Dip

Extend both hands and one leg forward, balancing on the other leg. Lower the body to sit on the heel and return without losing the balance or touching the floor with any part of the body. Try with the other foot.

Balance Jump

With hands and arms out to the sides and body parallel to the ground, extend one leg back and balance the weight on the other leg. Quickly change balance to the other foot, maintaining the initial position but with the feet exchanged. Keep the body parallel to the ground during the change of legs. Try with arms outstretched forward.

Seat Balance

Sit on the floor, holding the ankles in front, with elbows inside the knees. The feet are flat on the floor, and the knees are bent at approximately a right angle. Raise the legs (toes pointed) so that the knees are straight, and balance on the seat for 5 seconds.

Individual Stunts
Heelstand

Begin in a full-squat position with the arms dangling at the sides. Jump upward to full leg extension with the weight on both heels and fling the arms out diagonally. Hold momentarily, then return to position. Several movements can be done rhythmically in succession.

Wicket Walk

Bend over and touch the floor with the weight evenly distributed on the hands and feet, thus forming a wicket. Walk the wicket forward, backward, and sideward.

Knee Jump to Standing

Kneel, with seat touching the heels and toes pointing backward (shoelaces against the floor). Jump to a standing position with a vigorous upward swing of the arms. It is easier to jump from a smooth floor than from a mat, because the toes slide more readily on the floor.

Partner and Group Stunts
Rowboat

Partners sit on the floor or on a mat, facing each other with legs apart and feet touching. Both grasp a wand with both hands. Pretend to row a boat. Seek a wide range of movement in the forward-backward rowing motion.

Wheelbarrow

One partner gets down on the hands with feet extended to the rear and legs apart. The other partner (the pusher) grasps partner's legs about halfway between the ankles and the knees. The wheelbarrow walks forward on the hands, supported by the pusher. Movements should be under good control.

All tumbling and inverted balances should be done on tumbling mat.

Children who have difficulty with the Cartwheel should be instructed to concentrate on taking the weight of the body on the hands in succession (like the spokes of a wheel). They need to get the feel of the weight support and later can concentrate on getting the body into proper position. After the class has had some practice in doing Cartwheels, a running approach with a skip can be added before takeoff.

Working in pairs can be helpful. One student critiques the other's performance to make sure that the key performance and safety areas are addressed.

After the activities are learned, place emphasis on correct performance emphasizing three phases:
1. Starting position
2. Execution
3. Finishing position

Keep the arms and legs as nearly vertical as possible when doing the Wicket Walk. A common error in the execution of this stunt is to keep the hands positioned too far forward of the feet.

The stunt can be done without a wand by having children grasp hands.

Children have a tendency to grasp the legs too near the feet. The pusher must not push too fast. The wheelbarrow should have the head up and look forward. The pusher should carry the legs low and keep the arms extended.

Game Activity

Partner Stoop

Supplies: Music

Skills: Marching rhythmically

The game follows the same basic principle of stooping as in Circle Stoop, but it is played with partners. The group forms a double circle, with partners facing counterclockwise, which means that one partner is on the inside and one is on the outside. When the music begins, all march in the line of direction. After a short period of marching, a signal (whistle) is sounded, and the inside circle reverses direction and marches the other way--clockwise. The partners are thus separated. When the music stops, the outer circle stands still, and the partners making up the inner circle walk to rejoin their respective outer circle partners. As soon as a child reaches her partner, they join inside hands and stoop without losing balance. The last couple to stoop and those who have lost balance go to the center of the circle and wait out the next round.

Insist that players walk when joining their partner. This avoids the problem of stampeding and colliding with others.

Crows and Cranes

Supplies: None

Skills: Running, dodging

Two goal lines are drawn about 50 ft apart. Children are divided into two groups—the crows and the cranes. The groups face each other at the center of the area, about 5 ft apart. The leader calls out either "Crows" or "Cranes," using a cr-r-r-r-r sound at the start of either word to mask the result. If "Crows" is the call, the crows chase the cranes to the goal line. If "Cranes" is the call, then the cranes chase. Any child caught goes over to the other side. The team that has the most players when the game ends is the winner.

Lesson Plans for Grades 3-4 - Week 23
Manipulative Skills Using Wands and Hoops

Objectives:
To participate in aerobic fitness activities for an extended time
To understand proper technique for isometric exercises
To demonstrate the ability to cooperate and compete in game activities
To manipulate and control a hoop in a variety of challenges

Equipment Required:
One wand for each student
One hoop for each student
Tom-tom
Music and signs for aerobic exercises
Cones pinnies and fleece balls for games

Instructional Activities	Teaching Hints

Introductory Activity -- European Rhythmic Running with Variations

Students clap to the beat of the drum and run in single-file formation. Practice some of the following variations:
1. Clap hands the first beat of a four beat rhythm.
2. Stamp foot and clap hands on the first beat.
3. On signal, make a complete turn, using four running steps.

Encourage students to originate different variations of rhythmic running.

After the rhythm is learned, stop striking the drumbeat and let the class maintain the rhythm.

Fitness Development Activity -- Aerobic Fitness

The following aerobic movements are suggestions only. Also, stop the aerobic fitness movements and do flexibility and strength development activity to allow students time to recover aerobically.
1. Rhythmic run with clap
2. Bounce turn and clap
3. Rhythmic 4-count curl-ups (knees, toes, knees, back)
4. Rhythmic Crab Kicks (slow time)
5. Jumping Jack combination
6. Double knee lifts
7. Lunges (right, left, forward) with single-arm circles (on the side lunges) and double-arms circles (on the forward lunge)
8. Rhythmic trunk twists
9. Directional run (forward, backward, side, turning)
10. Rock side to side with clap
11. Side leg raises (alternate legs)
12. Rhythmic 4-count push-ups (If these are too difficult for students, substitute single-arm circles in the push-up position.)

See text, p. 191-195 for descriptions of aerobic activities.

Use music to stimulate effort. Any combination of movements can be used.

Keep the steps simple and easy to perform. Some students will become frustrated if the learning curve is steep.

Signs which explain the aerobic activities will help students remember performance cues.

Don't stress or expect perfection. Allow students to perform the activities as best they can.

Alternate bouncing and running movements with flexibility and strength development movements.

Lesson Focus -- Manipulative Skills Using Wands and Hoops

Select activities from the each of the exercises and challenges groups.
Strength Exercises with Wands
1. Pull the Wand Apart. Place the hands 6 inches apart near the center of the wand. With a tight grip to prevent slippage and with arms extended, pull the hands apart. Change grip and position.
2. Push the Wand Together. Hold the wand as previously, except push the hands together.
3. Wand Twist. Hold the wand with both hands about 6 inches apart. Twist the hands in opposite directions.
4. Bicycle. Holding the wand horizontally throughout and using an overhand grip, extend the wand outward and downward. Bring it upward near the body, completing a circular movement. On the downward movement, push the wand together, and on the upward movement, pull the wand apart.
5. Arm Spreader. Hold the wand overhead with hands spread wide. Attempt to compress the stick. Reverse force, and attempt to pull the stick apart.
6. Dead Lift. Partially squat and place the wand under the thighs. Place the hands between the legs and try to lift. Try also with hands on the outside of the legs.

Wands can be made from ¾ inch maple dowels or from a variety of broom and mop handles. They should be cut to a length of 36 inches. Wands are noisy when they hit the floor. Putting rubber crutch tips on the ends of a wand alleviates most of the noise and makes them easier to pick up.

The isometric exercises with wands presented can be performed with a variety of grips. With the wand horizontal, use either the overhand or underhand grip. With the wand in vertical position, grip with the thumbs pointed up, down, or toward each other.

7. Abdominal Tightener. While standing, place the wand behind the buttocks. Pull forward on the ends of the wand and resist with the abdominal muscles.

Stretching Exercises with Wands

1. Side Bender. Grip the wand and extend the arms overhead with feet apart. Bend sideways as far as possible, maintaining straight arms and legs. Recover, and bend to the other side.
2. Body Twist. Place the wand behind the neck, with arms draped over the wand from behind. Rotate the upper body first to the right as far as possible and then to the left. The feet and hips should remain in position. The twist is at the waist.
3. Body Twist to Knee. Assume body twist position. Bend the trunk forward and twist so that the right end of the wand touches the left knee. Recover, and touch the left end to the right knee.
4. Shoulder Stretcher. Grip the wand at the ends in a regular grip. Extend the arms overhead and rotate the wand, arms, and shoulders backward until the stick touches the back of the legs. The arms should be kept straight. Those who find the stretch too easy should move their hands closer to the center of the wand.
5. Toe Touch. Grip the wand with the hands about shoulder width apart. Bend forward, reaching down as far as possible without bending the knees. The movement should be slow and controlled. Try the same activity from a sitting position.
6. Over the Toes. Sit down, flex the knees, place the wand over the toes, and rest it against the middle of the arch. Grip the stick with the fingers at the outside edge of the feet. Slowly extend the legs forward, pushing against the stick and trying for a full extension of the legs.

Wand Challenges

1. Can you reach down and pick up your wand without bending your knees?
2. Try to balance your wand on different body parts. Watch the top of the wand to get cues on how to retain the balance.
3. Can you hold your stick against the wall and move over it? Gradually raise the height of the wand.
4. Let's see whether you can hold the stick at both ends and move through the gap.
5. Can you twirl the wand and keep it going like a windmill?
6. Let's see how many different ways you can move over and around your wand when it is on the floor.
7. Put one end of the wand on the floor and hold the other end. How many times can you run around your wand without getting dizzy?
8. Place one end of the wand against a wall. Holding the other end and keeping the wand against the wall, duck underneath. Place the wand lower and lower on the wall and go under.
9. Place the wand between your feet and hop around as though you are on a pogo stick.
10. Toss the wand from one hand to the other.
11. Hold the wand vertically near the middle. Can you release your grip and catch the wand before it falls to the floor?
12. Have a partner hold a wand horizontally above the floor. Jump, leap, and hop over the wand. Gradually raise the height of the wand.
13. Put your wand on the floor and try making different kinds of bridges over it.
14. Place the wand on the floor. Curl alongside it, just touching it. Curl at one end of the wand.
15. Balance the wand vertically on the floor. Release the wand and try to complete different stunts--clapping the hands, doing a heel click, touching different body parts--before the wand falls to the floor.
16. Put the wand on the floor and see how many ways you can push it, using different body parts.

Hoop Activities

1. Hula-hoop using various body parts such as waist, neck, knees, arms and fingers.
   a. While hula-hooping on the arms, try to change the hoop from one arm to the other.

Repeat each exercise with a different grip. Exercises can also be repeated with the wand in different positions: in front of the body (either horizontal or vertical), overhead, or behind the back. Hold each exercise for 8 to 12 seconds.

Be gentle when stretching. Reach and stretch the muscles, hold the stretch for a few seconds and relax. Repeat a number of times.

Because wands are noisy when dropped, youngsters should hold their wands with both hands or put them on the floor during instruction.

An adequate amount of space is needed for each individual because wand stunts demand room.

Children may easily be injured using wands improperly. Teach children proper use of wands. Emphasize the need to use care when handling wands to avoid injury to self and others. Do not allow any improper use of wands.

Hoop activities are noisy. The teacher may find it helpful to have the children lay their hoops on the floor when they are to listen.

b. Change hoop from one partner to another while hula-hooping.

c. Try leg-skippers--hula-hoop with one leg and jump the hoop with the other leg.

2. Jump-rope with the hoop--forward, sideways, and backward. Begin with a back-and-forth swing.

3. Roll hoop and run alongside it. Run in front of it.

4. Roll hoop with a reverse spin to make it return to the thrower.

5. Roll with a reverse spin and see how many times partner can go through it.

6. Balance the hoop on your head, try to walk through it ("thread the needle") forward, backward and sideways.

7. Try partner activities:

a. Play catch with hoop.

b. Hula-hoop on one arm, toss to partner who catches it on one arm.

c. Use two hoops for catching.

d. Hoop with one hoop and play catch with other.

e. Move through a hoop held by a partner.

In activities that require children to jump through hoops, instruct the holder to grasp the hoop lightly, so as not to cause an awkward fall if a performer hits it.

Hoops can serve as a "home" for various activities. For instance, children might leave their hoops to gallop in all directions and then return quickly to the hoop on command.

When teaching the reverse spin with hoops, have the students throw the hoop up, in place, rather than forward along the floor. After they learn the upward throw, they can progress to the forward throw for distance.

Game Activity

Home Base

Supplies: Cones to delineate the area, four pinnies

Skills: Reaction time, locomotor movements, body management

The area is divided into four quadrants with cones or floor lines. Each quadrant is the home base for one of the squads. The captain of the squad wears a pinnie for easy identification. The teams begin in a straight line sitting on the floor. The teacher calls out a locomotor movement which the players use to move throughout the area. When the teacher calls "Home base," the students return to their quadrant and return to the starting position behind their captain. The first team to return to proper position (sitting in a straight line) is awarded 2 points. Second place receives 1 point.

Teaching suggestion: Avoid calling "Home base" until the students have left the area of their quadrant. A number of different formations can be specified which students must assume upon return to their home base.

Indianapolis 500

Supplies: None

Skills: Running, tagging

Children start in a large circle and are numbered off in threes or fours. A race starter says "Start your engines," and then calls out a number. Those children with the corresponding number run clockwise around the circle and try to tag players in front of them. If the leader yells "Pit stop," all runners have to stop and return to their original position. If "Accident" is called by the leader, all runners must change direction and proceed counterclockwise. Change the starter often.

Nine Lives

Supplies: Fleece balls

Skills: Throwing, dodging

Any number of fleece balls can be used--the more the better. At a signal, players get a ball and hit as many people below waist level as possible. When a player counts that she has been hit nine times, she leaves the game and stands out of bounds until she has counted to 25. A player may run anywhere with a ball or to get a ball, but he may possess only one ball at a time. Players must not be hit in the head. This puts the thrower out.

Teaching suggestion: Children often cheat about the number of times they have been hit. A few words about fair play may be necessary, but a high degree of activity is the important game element.

Variations:

1. For a ball caught on the fly, a designated number of hits may be taken away.

2. Either left- or right-hand throwing can be specified.

Lesson Plans for Grades 3-4 - Week 24
Rhythmic Movement (3)

Objectives:
To develop personal aerobic fitness activities
To perform locomotor movements to rhythm
To understand strategies in simple game activities

Equipment Required:
Music for rhythmic activities
Tinikling poles
Clubs and balls for game
Jump the shot rope
Beachballs

Instructional Activities	Teaching Hints

Introductory Activity -- Tortoise and Hare

When the leader calls out the word "tortoise," students run in place slowly. On the word "hare," they change to a rapid run. Students can work in small groups to allow for more leaders.

Try some different variations such as:
1. Moving throughout the area.
2. Performing various stretching activities.
3. Moving in different directions.

Fitness Development Activity -- Aerobic Fitness

1. Rhythmic run with clap
2. Bounce turn and clap
3. Rhythmic 4-count curl-ups (knees, toes, knees, back)
4. Rhythmic Crab Kicks (slow time)
5. Jumping Jack combination
6. Double knee lifts
7. Lunges (right, left, forward) with single-arm circles (on the side lunges) and double-arms circles (on the forward lunge)
8. Rhythmic trunk twists
9. Directional run (forward, backward, side, turning)
10. Rock side to side with clap
11. Side leg raises (alternate legs)
12. Rhythmic 4-count push-ups (If these are too difficult for students, substitute single-arm circles in the push-up position.)

See text, p. 191-195 for descriptions of aerobic activities.

Use music to stimulate effort. Any combination of movements can be used.

Keep the steps simple and easy to perform. Some students will become frustrated if the learning curve is steep.

Signs which explain the aerobic activities will help students remember performance cues.

Don't stress or expect perfection. Allow students to perform the activities as best they can.

Alternate bouncing and running movements with flexibility and strength development movements.

Lesson Focus -- Rhythmic Movement (3)

Begin each lesson with a review of one or two dances youngsters know and enjoy. Review dances from lesson plans #11 and #16 as desired before teaching new ones.

Rhythms should be taught like other sport skills. Avoid striving for perfection so students know it is acceptable to make mistakes. Teach a variety of dances rather than one or two in depth in case some students find it difficult to master a specific dance. Make dances easy for students to learn by implementing some of the following techniques:
1. Teach the dances without using partners.
2. Allow youngsters to move in any direction without left-right orientation.
3. Use scattered formation instead of circles.
4. Emphasize strong movements such as clapping and stamping to increase involvement.
5. Play the music at a slower speed when first learning the dance.

When introducing a dance, use the following methodology:
1. Tell about the dance and listen to the music.
2. Clap the beat and learn the verse.
3. Practice the dance steps without the music and with verbal cues.
4. Practice the dance with the music.

Records can be ordered from Wagon Wheel Records, 17191 Corbina Lane #203, Huntington Beach, CA (714) 846-8169.

E-Z Mixer

Record: GR 2204

Formation: Circle formation with couples in promenade position, inside hands joined, facing counterclockwise.

Directions:

Measures	Action
1--2	With partner B on the right, walk forward four steps. (Forward, 2, 3, 4) Back out to face center in a single circle. (Circle, 2, 3, 4)
3--4	Partners B walk to the center. (In, 2, 3, 4) Back out of the center. (Out, 2, 3, 4)
5--6	Partners A take four steps to the center, turning one half left face on the fourth step. (In, 2, 3, turn left face) They take four steps toward the corner. (Out, 2, 3, 4)
7--8	As swing the corner B twice around, opening up to face counterclockwise, back in starting position, to begin the dance again. (Swing, 2, 3, open)

Irish Washerwoman (Irish)

Records: LS E-11, E-22; MAV 1043

Formation: Single circle, couples facing center, partner B to the right, hands joined

Directions: Dancers follow the call.

Call	Action
All join hands and go to the middle.	Beginning left, take four steps to the center. (Center, 2, 3, 4)
And with your big foot keep time to the fiddle.	Stamp four times in place (Stamp, 2, 3, 4)
And when you get back, remember my call.	Take four steps backward to place (Back, 2, 3, 4)
Swing your corner and promenade all.	Swing the corner and promenade in the line of direction. (Swing, 2, 3, promenade)

Dancers keep promenading until they hear the call again to repeat the pattern.

Any piece of music with a moderate 4/4 rhythm is appropriate for this basic mixer.

Gustaf's Skoal (Swedish)

Records: HLP 4027; LS E-11, E-22; MAV 1044; RPT 107

Formation: The formation is similar to a square dance set of four couples, each facing center. Partner A is to the left of partner B. Couples join inside hands; the outside hand is on the hip. Two of the couples facing each other are designated the head couples. The other two couples, also facing each other, are the side couples.

Directions: The dance is in two parts. During Part I, the music is slow and stately. The dancers perform with great dignity. The music for Part II is light and represents fun.

Measures	Part I Action
1--2	The head couples, inside hands joined, walk forward three steps and bow to the opposite couple. (Forward, 2, 3, bow)
3--4	The head couples take three steps backward to place and bow to each other. (The side couples hold their places during this action.) (Back, 2, 3, bow)
5--8	The side couples repeat action of measures 1—4 while the head couples hold their places. (Forward, 2, 3, bow; Back, 2, 3, bow)
9--16	The dancers repeat measures 1--8.

Measures	Part II Action
17--22	The side couples raise joined hands to form an arch. Head couples skip forward four steps, release partners' hands, join inside hands with opposite person, and skip under the nearest arch with new partner. After going under the arch, they drop hands and head back home to their original partner. (Head couples: Skip, 2, 3, 4; Under, 2, 3, 4; Around, 2, 3, 4)
23--24	All couples join both hands with partners and swing once around with four skipping steps. (Swing, 2, 3, 4)
25--30	Head couples form arches while side couples repeat the action of measures 17--22. (Side couples: Skip, 2, 3, 4; Under, 2, 3, 4; Around, 2, 3, 4)
31--32	All couples then repeat the movements in measures 23--24. (Swing, 2, 3, 4)

Tinikling (Philippine Islands)

Records: KIM 8095, 9015; MAV 1047

Formation: Sets of fours scattered around the room. Each set has two strikers and two dancers (Figure 16.6).

Directions:

Two 8-foot bamboo poles and two crossbars on which the poles rest are needed for the dance. A striker kneels at each end of the poles; both strikers hold the end of a pole in each hand. The music is in waltz meter, 3/4 time, with an accent on the first beat. The strikers slide and strike the poles together on count 1. On the other two beats of the waltz measure, the poles are opened about 15 inches apart, lifted an inch or so, and tapped twice on the crossbars in time to counts 2 and 3. The rhythm "close, tap, tap" is continued throughout the dance, each sequence constituting a measure.

Basically, the dance requires that a step be done outside the poles on the close (count 1) and that two steps be done inside the poles (counts 2 and 3) when the poles are tapped on the crossbars. Many step combinations have been devised. The basic tinikling step should be practiced until it is mastered. The step is done singly, although two dancers are performing. Each dancer takes a position at an opposite end and on the opposite side so that the dancer's right side is to the bamboo poles.

Count 1: Step slightly forward with the left foot.
Count 2: Step with the right foot between the poles.
Count 3: Step with the left foot between the poles.
Count 4: Step with the right outside to dancer's own right.
Count 5: Step with the left between the poles.
Count 6: Step with the right between the poles.
Count 7: Step with the left outside to the original position.

The initial step (count 1) is used only to get the dance under way. The last step (count 7) to original position is actually the beginning of a new series (7, 8, 9--10, 11, 12).

Tinikling steps also can be adjusted to 4/4 rhythm (close, close, tap, tap), which requires the poles to be closed on two counts and open on the other two. The basic foot pattern is two steps outside the poles and two inside. For the sake of conformity, we present all routines in the original 3/4 time (close, tap, tap). If other rhythms are used, adjust accordingly.

Dancers can go from side to side, or can return to the side from which they entered. The dance can be done singly, with the two dancers moving in opposite directions from side to side, or the dancers can enter from and leave toward the same side. Dancers can do the same step patterns or do different movements. They can dance as partners, moving side by side with inside hands joined, or facing each other with both hands joined.

Teaching suggestions:

Steps should be practiced first with stationary poles or with lines drawn on the floor. Jump ropes can be used as stationary objects over which to practice. Students handling the poles should concentrate on watching each other rather than the dancer to avoid becoming confused by the dancer's feet.

To gain a sense of the movement pattern for 3/4 time, slap both thighs with the hands on the "close," and clap the hands twice for movements inside the poles. For 4/4 time, slap the right thigh with the right hand, then the left thigh with the left hand, followed by two claps. This routine should be done to music, with the poles closing and opening as indicated. Getting the feel of the rhythm is important.

Game Activity

Jump the Shot
Supplies: A jump-the-shot rope
Skill: Rope jumping

The players stand in circle formation. One player with a long rope stands in the center. A soft object is tied to the free end of the rope to give it some weight. An old, deflated ball or beanbag makes a good weight (tie the rope to it and use duct tape to keep it from becoming untied). The center player turns the rope under the feet of the circle players, who must jump over it. A player who touches the rope with the feet must move up to the next group.

Variation: Change the center player after one or two misses. The center player should be cautioned to keep the rope along the ground. The rope speed can be varied. A good way to turn the rope is to sit cross-legged and turn it over the head. Different tasks can be performed such as hopping, jumping and turning, or jumping and clapping.

Variations: 1. Squads line up in spoke formation. Each member does a specified number of jumps (from three to five) and then exits. The next squad member in line must come in immediately without missing a turn of the rope. A player scores a point for the squad when he comes in on time, jumps the prescribed number of turns, and exits successfully. The squad with the most points wins.

2. Couples line up in the same formation. They join inside hands and stand side by side when jumping.

Beachball Batball
Supplies: Four to six beachballs
Skills: Batting, tactile handling

Two games are played across the gymnasium area. The teams are scattered throughout the area without restriction as to where they may move. To begin the game, the balls are placed on the centerline dividing the court area. Four to six beachballs are in play at the same time. A score occurs when the beachball is batted over the end line. Once the ball moves across the end line it is dead. Players concentrate on the remaining balls in play.

If a ball is on the floor, it is picked up and batted into play. At no time may a ball be carried. After all four balls are scored, the game ends. A new game is started after teams switch goals.

Club Guard

Supplies: A juggling club or bowling pin and foam rubber ball

Skill: Throwing

A circle about 15 ft in diameter is drawn. Inside the circle at the center, an 18-in. circle is drawn. The club is put in the center of the small circle. One child guards the club. The other children stand outside the large circle, which is the restraining line for them.

The circle players throw the ball at the club and try to knock it down. The guard tries to block the throws with the legs and body. She must, however, stay out of the small inner circle. The outer circle players pass the ball around rapidly so that one of the players can get an opening to throw, since the guard needs to maneuver to protect the club. Whoever knocks down the club becomes the new guard. If the guard steps into the inner circle, she loses the place to whoever has the ball at that time.

Teaching suggestion: A small circle cut from plywood (or a hula hoop or similar object) makes a definite inner circle so that determining whether the guard steps inside is easier. The outer circle should also be definite.

Variation: More than one club can be in the center.

Lesson Plans for Grades 3-4 - Week 25
Volleyball-Related Skills (1)

Objectives:
To perform overhand and underhand volleyball passing skills
To volley the ball a number of times against a wall
To practice skills successfully with a partner
To learn the basic rules of volleyball

Equipment Required:
Tambourine
One beachball, 8" foam rubber, or
    volleyball trainer for each student
Volleyball net (6 ft height)
Music for exercises

Instructional Activities	Teaching Hints

Introductory Activity -- Bend, Stretch and Shake

Students should alternate between various bending and stretching activities. On signal, students shake and relax various body parts. Teach a variety of bending and stretching activities.

Use a tambourine to signal changes in bending and stretching. Shake it to signal shaking activities.

Fitness Development Activity -- Astronaut Drills

Walk while doing Arm circles	30 seconds	Tape alternating segments of silence and music to signal duration of exercise. Music segments indicate aerobic activity while intervals of silence announce flexibility and strength development activities.
Crab Alternate-Leg Extension	35 seconds	
Skip	30 seconds	
Body Twist	35 seconds	
Slide	30 seconds	
Jumping Jack Variations	35 seconds	
Crab Walk to center and back	30 seconds	
Abdominal Challenges	35 seconds	Use scatter formation; ask students to change directions from time to time in order to keep spacing.
Hop to center and back	30 seconds	
Push-Up Challenges	35 seconds	
Gallop	30 seconds	
Bear Hugs	35 seconds	Allow students to adjust the workload pace.
Pogo Stick Jump	30 seconds	

Cool down with stretching and walking or jogging for 1-2 minutes.

See text, p. 174-186 for descriptions of exercises.

Lesson Focus -- Volleyball-Related Skills (1)

Skills
Practice the following skills:
Overhand Pass

    To execute an overhand pass, the player moves underneath the ball and controls it with the fingertips. The cup of the fingers is made so that the thumbs and forefingers are close together and the other fingers are spread. The hands are held forehead high, with elbows out and level with the floor. The player, when in receiving position, looks ready to shout upward through the hands. The player contacts the ball above eye level and propels it with the force of spread fingers, not with the palms. At the moment of contact, the legs are straightened and the hands and arms follow through.

Forearm Pass (Underhand Pass)

    The hands are clasped together so that the forearms are parallel. The clasp should be relaxed, with the type of handclasp a matter of choice. The thumbs are kept parallel and together, and the fingers of one hand make a partially cupped fist, with the fingers of the other hand overlapping the fist. The wrists are turned downward and the elbow joints are reasonably locked. The forearms are held at the proper angle to rebound the ball, with contact made with the fists or forearms between the knees as the receiver crouches.

Using beach balls and trainer volleyballs will allow youngsters time to move into the path of the volleyball instead of reaching for the ball. Proper footwork is critical to the success of volleyball; using proper balls will help assure that youngsters learn correctly.

Instructional cues of passing include the following:
1. Move into the path of the ball; don't reach for it.
2. Bend the knees prior to making contact.
3. Contact the ball with the fingertips (overhand pass).
4. Extend the knees upon contact with the ball.
5. Follow through after striking the ball.

Individual Passing Drills

1. Practice wall rebounding: Stand 6 feet away from a wall. Pass the ball against the wall and catch it.
2. From a spot 6 feet from the wall, throw the ball against the wall and alternate an overhand pass with a forearm pass.
3. Throw the ball to one side (right or left) and move to the side to pass the ball to the wall. Catch the rebound.
4. Pass the ball directly overhead and catch it. Try making two passes before catching the ball. Later, alternate an overhand pass with a forearm pass and catch the ball. This is a basic drill and should be mastered before proceeding to others.

Partner Passing Drills

1. Players are about 10 feet apart. Play A tosses the ball (controlled toss) to player B, who passes the ball back to A, who catches the ball. Continue for several exchanges and then change throwers.
2. Two players are about 15 feet apart. Player a passes to themselves first and then makes a second pass to player B, who catches the ball and repeats. Follow with a return by B.
3. Players A and B try to keep the ball in the air continuously.
4. Players are about 15 feet apart. Player A remains stationary and passes in such a fashion that player B must move from side to side. An option is to have player B move forward and backward.
5. Players are about 10 feet apart. Both have hoops and attempt to keep one foot in the hoop while passing. Try keeping both feet in the hoop.
6. Player A passes to player B and does a complete turnaround. B passes back to A and also does a full turn. Other stunts can be used.

The usual basketball court should be divided into two volleyball courts on which players play crosswise. Nets should be lowered to 6 feet and raised 6 to 12 inches as children mature.

In the primary grades, children should have had ball-handling experiences related to volleyball skills. Rebounding and controlling balloons is an excellent related experience, particularly for younger children. Included in ball-handling experiences with beach balls or foam rubber training balls should be exploratory work in batting with the hands and other body parts.

Regulation volleyballs should not be used with third and fourth grade students. An 8-inch foam rubber training ball has much the same feel as a volleyball but does not cause pain. The foam balls should be used for skill practice. Another excellent ball is the volleyball trainer which closely resembles a volleyball but is larger in diameter and lighter in weight. Either ball helps keep children from developing a fear of the fast-moving object.

Game Activity -- Volleyball Lead-Up Games

Beachball Volleyball

Supplies: A beach ball 16 to 20 inches in diameter
Skills: Most passing skills, modified serving

The players of each team are in two lines on their respective sides of the net. Serving is done, as in regulation volleyball, by the player on the right side of the back line. The distance is shortened, however, because serving a beach ball successfully from the normal volleyball serving distance is difficult. The player serves from the normal playing position on the court in the right back position. Scoring is as in regulation volleyball. Play continues until the ball touches the floor.

A team loses a point to the other team when it fails to return the ball over the net by the third volley or when it returns the ball over the net but the ball hits the floor out-of-bounds without being touched by the opposing team. The server continues serving as long as she scores. Rotation is as in regulation volleyball.

Teaching suggestion: The server must be positioned as close to the net as possible while still remaining in the right back position on the court. Successful serving is an important component of an enjoyable game.

Variations:

1. In a simplified version of the game, the ball is put into play by one player in the front line, who throws the ball into the air and then passes it over the net. Play continues until the ball touches the floor, but the ball may be volleyed any number of times before crossing the net. When either team has scored 5 points, the front and back lines of the respective teams change. When the score reaches 10 for the leading team, the lines change back. Game is 15.

2. Any player in the back line may catch the ball as it comes initially from the opposing team and may immediately make a little toss and pass the ball to a teammate. The player who catches the ball and bats it cannot send it across the net before a teammate has touched it.

Informal Volleyball

Supplies: A trainer volleyball
Skills: Passing

This game is similar to regulation volleyball, but there is no serving. Each play begins with a student on one side tossing to herself and passing the ball high over the net. Points are scored for every play, as there is no "side out." As soon as a point is scored, the nearest player takes the ball and immediately puts it into play. Otherwise, basic volleyball rules govern the game. Rotation occurs as soon as a team has scored 5 points, with the front and back lines changing place. Action is fast, and the game moves rapidly since every play scores a point for one team or the other.

Lesson Plans for Grades 3-4 - Week 26
Volleyball Related Skills (2)

Objectives:
To perform overhand and underhand volleyball passing skills
To volley the ball a number of times against a wall
To hit an underhand serve over a 6' net
To learn the basic rules of volleyball

Equipment Required:
Music for exercises
One beachball, 8" foam rubber, or
    volleyball trainer for each student
Volleyball net (6 ft height)

Instructional Activities	Teaching Hints

Introductory Activity -- Move, Perform Task

Move around the area using any desired locomotor movement; on signal, stop and perform a task such as an exercise or stunt. Some suggested activities are: Heel Click, Push-Up, Stork Stand, Sit-up, or any desired stretch.

Allow students to demonstrate novel responses in order to increase the range of student response.

Fitness Development Activity -- Astronaut Drills

Walk while doing Arm circles	30 seconds	
Crab Alternate-Leg Extension	35 seconds	
Skip	30 seconds	
Body Twist	35 seconds	
Slide	30 seconds	
Jumping Jack Variations	35 seconds	
Crab Walk to center and back	30 seconds	
Abdominal Challenges	35 seconds	
Hop to center and back	30 seconds	
Push-Up Challenges	35 seconds	
Gallop	30 seconds	
Bear Hugs	35 seconds	
Pogo Stick Jump	30 seconds	

Cool down with stretching and walking or jogging for 1-2 minutes.

See text, p. 194-195 for description of Astronaut Drills.

Tape alternating segments of silence and music to signal duration of exercise. Music segments indicate aerobic activity (30 seconds) while intervals of silence (35 seconds) announce flexibility and strength development activities.

Use scatter formation; ask students to change directions from time to time in order to keep spacing.

Allow students to adjust the workload pace. They should be allowed to move at a pace that is consistent with their ability level.

Lesson Focus -- Volleyball Related Skills (2)

Skills
Review skills taught in the previous week:
Overhand Pass
Forearm Pass (Underhand pass)

Introduce a new skill:
Underhand Serve

    Directions are for a right-handed serve. The player stands facing the net with the left foot slightly forward and the weight on the right (rear) foot. The ball is held in the left hand with the left arm across and a little in front of the body. On the serving motion, the server steps forward with the left foot, transferring the weight to the front foot, and at the same time brings the right arm back in a preparatory motion. The right hand now swings forward and contacts the ball just below center. The ball can be hit with an open hand or with the fist (facing forward or sideward). Children should explore the best way to strike the ball, with the flat of the hand or the fist. Each player can select the method that is personally most effective.

Drills
Individual Passing Drills
1. Pass the ball 3 feet or so to one side, move under the ball, and pass it back to the original spot. The next pass should be to the other side.
2. Pass the ball directly overhead. On the return, jump as high as possible and make a second pass. Continue.
3. Stand with one foot in a hoop. Pass the ball overhead and attempt to continue passing while keeping one foot in the hoop. Try with both feet in the hoop.

The serve is used to start play. The underhand serve is easiest for elementary school children to learn even though the overhand (floater) serve is the most effective. Few youngsters will be capable of mastering the overhand serve.

The following instructional cues focus on correct performance of the serve:

1. Use opposition. Place the opposite foot of the serving hand forward.

2. Transfer the weight to the forward foot.

3. Keep the eyes on the ball.

4. Decide prior to the serve where it should be placed.

5. Follow through; don't punch at the ball.

Partner Passing Drills:
1. Players are about 15 feet apart. Player A remains stationary and passes in such a fashion that player B must move from side to side. An option is to have player B move forward and backward.
2. Players are about 10 feet apart. Both have hoops and attempt to keep one foot in the hoop while passing. Try keeping both feet in the hoop.
3. Player A passes to player B and does a complete turnaround. B passes back to A and also does a full turn. Other stunts can be used.

Partner Serving and Passing Drills
1. Partners are about 20 feet apart. Partner A serves to partner B, who catches the ball and returns the serve to partner A.
2. Partner A serves to partner B, who makes a pass back to partner A. Change responsibilities.
3. Service One-Step. Partners begin about 10 feet apart. Partner A serves to partner B, who returns the serve with partner A catching. If there is no error and if neither receiver moved the feet to catch, both players take one step back. This is repeated each time no error or foot movement by the receivers occur. If an error occurs or if appreciable foot movement is evident, the players revert to the original distance of 10 feet and start over.

It is difficult for third and fourth grade students to use regulation volleyballs. An 8-inch foam rubber training ball has much the same feel as a volleyball but does not cause pain. The foam balls should be used for skill practice. Another excellent ball is the volleyball trainer which closely resembles a volleyball but is larger in diameter and lighter in weight. Either ball helps keep children from developing a fear of the fast-moving object.

The use of the fist to hit balls on normal returns causes poor control and interrupts play. Except for dig passes, both hands should be used to return the ball. Teachers should rule hitting with the fist a loss of a point if the practice persists.

Game Activity - Volleyball Lead-Up Games

Continue playing the games listed in the Lesson Plan 25. The lead-up games for this age are:
  Beachball Volleyball
  Informal Volleyball

Introduce the following game:
Shower Service Ball
  Supplies: Four to six trainer volleyballs
  Skills: Serving, catching
  A line parallel to the net is drawn through the middle of each court to define the serving area. Players are scattered in no particular formation. The game involves the skills of serving and catching. To start the game, two or three volleyballs are given to each team and are handled by players in the serving area.
  Balls may be served at any time and in any order by a server who must be in the back half of the court. Any ball served across the net is to be caught by any player near the ball. The person catching or retrieving a ball moves quickly to the serving area and serves. A point is scored for a team whenever a served ball hits the floor in the other court or is dropped by a receiver. Two scorers are needed, one for each side.
Teaching suggestion: As children improve, all serves should be made from behind the baseline.

Lesson Plans for Grades 3-4 - Week 27
Manipulative Skills Using Paddles and Balls

Objectives:
To quickly assemble in a small group formation
To continuously jump a self-turned rope in a fitness setting
To know the proper method of holding a paddle
To hit a ball in a predetermined proper direction with a paddle

Equipment Required:
One paddle and ball for each student
One jump rope for each child
Bowling pins or clubs for game
Music for exercises
Rubber marking spots

Instructional Activities	Teaching Hints

Introductory Activity -- Find your Home

The class is divided in to teams of 5-6 players. One player in each group is designated the captain. Rubber spots are placed throughout the teaching area equal to the number of teams. Each spot serves as a home base for one of the squads. The teams begin in a straight line with the captain standing on a spot and the rest of the team lined up behind her. The teacher calls out a locomotor movement that the players use to move throughout the area. When the teacher calls "find your home!," each team lines up in starting formation with the captain first in line. The first team to return to proper position is awarded wins that round.

This is an excellent game to teach youngsters how to get in small group formations quickly.

If desired, use the call "find your home" to assemble the class in pre-assigned squads. Some teachers use squads for station teaching and dividing the class into teams.

Fitness Development Activity -- Continuity Drills

Rope Jumping - Forward	30 seconds	Students alternate jump rope activity with exercises done in two-count fashion. Exercises are done with the teacher saying "Ready;" the class answers "One-two" and performs a repetition of exercise. In activities like Push-Ups and Curl-Ups, allow students to pick any challenge activity they feel capable of performing. Teachers or students can lead.
Double Crab Kick	45 seconds	
Rope Jumping - Backward	30 seconds	
Knee Touch Curl-Up	45 seconds	
Jump and Slowly Turn Body	30 seconds	
Push-Up Challenges	45 seconds	
Rocker Step	30 seconds	
Bend and Twist	45 seconds	
Swing-Step Forward	30 seconds	
Side Flex	45 seconds	
Free Jumping	30 seconds	
Sit and Stretch	45 seconds	

See text, p. 194-195 for description of Astronaut Drills.

Allow students to adjust the workload to their level. This implies resting if the rope jumping is too strenuous.

Lesson Focus -- Manipulative Skills Using Paddles and Balls

1. Introduce proper method of holding paddle: forehand and backhand grip.
2. Place ball on paddle and attempt to roll it around the edge of the paddle without allowing it to fall off the paddle. Flip the paddle over and roll ball.
3. Balance the ball on the paddle using both right and left hands, as well as both grips while trying the following challenges:
   a. Touch the floor with hand.
   b. Move to knees and back to feet.
   c. Sit down and get back on feet.
   d. Lie down and get back on feet.
   e. Skip, gallop or any other locomotor movement.
4. Bounce the ball in the air using the paddle.
   a. See how many times it can be bounced without touching the floor.
   b. Bounce it off the paddle into the air and catch it with the other hand.
   c. Increase the height of the bounce.
   d. Kneel, sit down, other positions (student choice).
   e. Bounce ball off paddle, do a full turn and continue bouncing or balance ball on paddle.
   f. Bounce ball in the air, switch paddle to the other hand.

The use of plastic or wooden paddles and appropriate balls can be used to establish a basis for future play in racquetball, table tennis, squash, and regular tennis. These activities, particularly paddle tennis, take considerable space, so emphasis must be placed on controlled stroking rather than wild swinging.

Proper grip must be emphasized, and seeing that children maintain this is a constant battle. The easiest method to teach the proper grip is to have the student hold the paddle perpendicular to the floor and shake hands with it. Young people tend to revert to the inefficient hammer grip, so named because it is similar to the grip used on a hammer. Use the following instructional cues to improve paddle skills:

5. Dribble ball with the paddle.
   a. From a kneeling position.
   b. From a sitting position.
   c. From a standing position.
   d. Move in different directions--forward, sideways, circle.
   e. Move using different locomotor movements.
6. Alternate bouncing the ball in the air and on the floor.
7. Bounce ball of the paddle into the air and "catch" it with the paddle.
   a. Increase the height of the bounce.
   b. Perform a heel click, full turn or similar activity and catch the ball.
8. Bounce the ball continuously off the paddle into the air.
   a. Bounce the ball on the side of the paddle.
   b. Alternate sides of the paddle.
9. Place ball on the floor.
   a. Scoop it up with the paddle.
   b. Roll the ball and scoop it up with the paddle.
   c. Start dribbling the ball without touching it with hands.
10. Partner Activities.
   a. Begin partner activities with controlled throwing (feeding) by one partner and the designated stroke return by the other.
   b. Bounce ball back and forth. How many times can you bounce it back and forth to your partner without missing it?
   c. Increase the distance between partners and the height of the ball.
   d. Catch the ball on your paddle after throw from your partner, then return throw.
   e. Perform stunts while ball is in the air, such as catch ball behind back, under leg, above head, clap hands, heel clicks, full turns, etc.
   f. Use two balls.
   g. Move and keep the balls going; try skipping, hopping, jumping, sliding.

a. Hold the wrist reasonably stiff.

b. Use a smooth arm action.

c. Stroke through the ball and follow through.

d. Watch the ball strike the paddle. All paddles should have leather wrist thongs. The hand goes through the leather loop before grasping the paddle. No play should be permitted without this safety precaution.

Early learning activities should be practiced with both the right and the left hand The dominant hand should be developed more as youngsters begin to use the skills in game activities.

Game Activity

Steal the Treasure
   Supplies: A bowling pin
   Skill: Dodging
   A playing area 20 ft square is outlined, with a small circle in the center. A bowling pin placed in the circle is the treasure. A guard is set to protect the treasure. Players then enter the square and try to steal the treasure without getting caught. The guard tries to tag them. Anyone tagged must retire and wait for the next game. The player who gets the treasure is the next guard. Teaching suggestion: If getting the treasure seems too easy, the child can be required to carry the treasure to the boundary of the square without being tagged.
   Variation: <u>Bear and Keeper</u>. Instead of a treasure, a bear (seated cross-legged on the ground) is protected by a keeper. Anyone who touches the bear without being tagged becomes the new keeper, with the old keeper becoming the bear.

Trees
   Supplies: None
   Skills: Running, dodging
   Two parallel lines are drawn 60 ft apart. All players, except the one who is it, are on one side of the area. On the signal "Trees," the players run to the other side of the court. The tagger tries to tag as many as possible. Any player tagged becomes a tree, stopping where tagged and keeping both feet in place. He cannot move the feet but can tag any runners who come close enough. The child who is it continues to chase the players as they cross on signal until all but one are caught. This player becomes it for the next game.
   To speed up the action, two or more taggers may be chosen. Children cross from side to side only on the signal "Trees."

Lesson Plans for Grades 3-4 - Week 28
Stunts and Tumbling Skills (3)

Objectives:
To put together a combination of movements in a smooth and flowing manner
To support the body weight in a variety of settings
To work cooperatively with a partner

Equipment Required:
Tumbling Mats
One jump rope for each student
Music for exercises
4-6 beachballs for game

Instructional Activities	Teaching Hints

Introductory Activity -- Combination Movement Patterns

Explore some of the following movement combinations:
1. Run, leap and roll.
2. Run, collapse and roll.
3. Hop, turn around and shake.
4. Run, change direction and collapse.
5. Hop, make a shape in the air and balance.

Encourage a variety of responses

Try having students work in pairs and generate different combinations. They can mimic each other's ideas.

Fitness Development Activity – Continuity Drills

Rope Jumping - Forward	30 seconds
Double Crab Kick	45 seconds
Rope Jumping - Backward	30 seconds
Knee Touch Curl-Up	45 seconds
Jump and Slowly Turn Body	30 seconds
Push-Up Challenges	45 seconds
Rocker Step	30 seconds
Bend and Twist	45 seconds
Swing-Step Forward	30 seconds
Side Flex	45 seconds
Free Jumping	30 seconds
Sit and Stretch	45 seconds

See text, p. 194-195 for description of Astronaut Drills.

Students alternate jump rope activity with exercises done in two-count fashion. Exercises are done with the teacher saying "Ready;" the class answers "One-two" and performs a repetition of exercise. In activities like Push-Ups and Curl-Ups, allow students to pick any challenge activity they feel capable of performing. Teachers or students can lead.

Allow students to adjust the workload to their level. This implies resting if the rope jumping is too strenuous.

Lesson Focus – Stunts and Tumbling Skills (3)

Animal Movements

Double-Lame Dog

Support the body on one hand and one leg. Move forward in this position, maintaining balance. The distance should be short (5 to 10 feet), as this stunt is strenuous. Different leg-arm combinations should be employed such as cross-lateral movements (right arm with left leg and left arm with right leg).

Turtle

Hold the body in a wide push-up position with the feet apart and the hands widely spread. From this position, move in various directions, keeping the plane of the body always about the same distance from the floor. Movements of the hands and feet should occur in small increments only.

Walrus Slap

From the front-leaning rest position, push the body up in the air quickly by force of the arms, clap the hands together, and recover to position.

Tumbling and Inverted Balances

Forward Roll Combinations

Review the Forward Roll (lesson plan #). Combinations such as the following can be introduced.
   a. Do a Forward Roll preceded by a short run.
   b. Do two Forward Rolls in succession.
   c. Do a Forward Roll to a vertical jump in the air, and repeat.

Five groups of activities in this lesson ensure that youngsters receive a variety of experiences. Pick a few activities from each group and teach them alternately. For example, teach one or two animal movements, then a tumbling and inverted balance, followed by a balance stunt, etc. Give equal time to each group of activities

Youngsters can do the animal walks around their mats. Many of the activities in this unit do not have to be performed on the mat.

Balance Stunts

Seat Balance

Sit on the floor, holding the ankles in front, with elbows inside the knees. The feet are flat on the floor, and the knees are bent at approximately a right angle. Raise the legs (toes pointed) so that the knees are straight, and balance on the seat for 5 seconds.

Face-to-Knee Touch

Begin in a standing position with feet together. Placing the hands on the hips, balance on one foot, with the other leg extended backward. Bend the trunk forward and touch the knee of the supporting leg with the forehead. Recover to original position.

Finger Touch

Put the right hand behind the back with the index finger straight and pointed down. Grasp the right wrist with the left hand. From an erect position with the feet about 6 inches apart, squat down and touch the floor with the index finger. Regain the erect position without losing balance.

Individual Stunts

Stoop and Stretch

Hold a beanbag with both hands. Stand with heels against a line and feet about shoulder width apart. Keeping the knees straight, reach between the legs with the beanbag and place it as far back as possible. Reach back and pick it up with both hands.

Tanglefoot

Stand with heels together and toes pointed out. Bend the trunk forward and extend both arms down between the knees and around behind the ankles. Bring the hands around the outside of the ankles from behind and touch the fingers to each other. Hold for a 5-second count. Balance for 5 seconds without releasing the handclasp.

Egg Roll

In a sitting position, assume the same clasped-hands position as for Tanglefoot. Roll sideways over one shoulder, then to the back, then to the other shoulder, and finally back up to the sitting position. The movements are repeated in turn to make a full circle back to place.

Toe Touch Nose

From a sitting position on the floor, touch the toes of either foot to the nose with the help of both hands. Do first one foot and then the other. More flexible youngsters will be able to place the foot on top of the head or even behind the neck. Although this is a flexibility exercise, caution should be used; the leg can be forced too far.

Toe Tug Walk

Bend over and grasp the toes with thumbs on top. Keep the knees bent slightly and the eyes forward. Walk forward without losing the grip on the toes. Walk backward and sideward to provide more challenge.

Partner and Group Stunts

Camel Lift and Walk

In the wheelbarrow position, the wheelbarrow raises the seat as high as possible, forming a camel. Camels can lower themselves or walk in the raised position.

Dump the Wheelbarrow

Get into the wheelbarrow position. Lift the legs and return to normal position.

Scatter tumbling mats throughout the area so that there is little standing in line waiting for a turn.

Children who have difficulty with forward rolls should not have to do them.

A major concern for safety is the neck and back region. Overweight children are at greater risk and might be allowed to avoid tumbling and inverted balances.

Limit the number of children per mat to 3 or 4.

All tumbling and inverted balances should be done on a tumbling mat.

Working in pairs can be helpful. One student critiques the other's performance to make sure that the key performance and safety areas are addressed.

After the activities are learned, place emphasis on correct performance emphasizing three phases:
1. Starting position
2. Execution
3. Finishing position

The secret to the egg roll is a vigorous sideward movement to secure initial momentum. If mats are used, two should be placed side by side to cover the extent of the roll. (Some children can do this stunt better from a crossed-ankle position.)

Dromedary Walk

One child (the support) gets down on the hands and knees. The other child sits on the support, facing the rear, and fixes the legs around the support's chest. The top child leans forward, to grasp the back of the support's ankles. The top child's arms are reasonably extended. The support takes the weight off the knees and walks forward with the top child's help.

Centipede

One child, the stronger and larger individual, gets down on the hands and knees. The other child faces the same direction, places the hands about 2 feet in front of the support's, then places the legs and body on top of the support. The knees should be spread apart and the heels locked together. The centipede walks with the top child using hands only and the supporting child using both hands and feet. The support should gather the legs well under while walking and not be on the knees.

Game Activity

Trades

Supplies: None

Skills: Imagery, running, dodging

The class is divided into two teams of equal number, each of which has a goal line. One team, the chasers, remains behind its goal line. The other team, the runners, approaches from its goal line, marching to the following dialogue:

Runners: Here we come.

Chasers: Where from?

Runners: New Orleans.

Chasers: What's your trade?

Runners: Lemonade.

Chasers: Show us some.

Runners move up close to the other team's goal line and proceed to act out an occupation or a specific task that they have chosen previously. The opponents try to guess what the pantomime represents. On a correct guess, the running team must run back to its goal line chased by the others. Any runner tagged must join the chasers. The game is repeated with roles reversed. The team ending with the greater number of players is the winner.

Teaching suggestion: If a team has trouble guessing the pantomime, the other team should provide hints. Teams also should be encouraged to have a number of activities selected so that little time is consumed in choosing the next activity to be pantomimed.

Beachball Batball

Supplies: Four to six beachballs

Skills: Batting, tactile handling

Two games are played across the gymnasium area. The teams are scattered throughout the area without restriction as to where they may move. To begin the game, the balls are placed on the centerline dividing the court area. Four to six beachballs are in play at the same time. A score occurs when the beachball is batted over the end line. Once the ball moves across the end line it is dead. Players concentrate on the remaining balls in play.

If a ball is on the floor, it is picked up and batted into play. At no time may a ball be carried. After all four balls are scored, the game ends. A new game is started after teams switch goals.

Lesson Plans for Grades 3-4 - Week 29
Fundamental Skills Through Relay Activities

Objectives:
To participate cooperatively in relay activities
To demonstrate respect for individual differences
To appreciate the joy of participation
To compete fairly in a structured activity

Equipment Required:
Beanbags for relays and game
Cones to mark lanes for relays
Exercise to Music Tape
Tambourine

Instructional Activities	Teaching Hints

Introductory Activity -- European Rhythmic Running with Equipment

Review European Rhythmic Running and emphasize the following points:
1. Move to·the rhythm.
2. Lift the knees and perform a trotting step.
3. Maintain proper spacing between each other.

After the review, give each child a beanbag or playground ball. Every fourth step, they can toss up the bag or bounce the ball. Other variations can be tried using different beats of the rhythm.

Fitness Development Activity -- Exercises to Music

Side Flex (switch sides)	30 seconds
Jogging	25 seconds
Abdominal Challenges	30 seconds
Slide or Skip	25 seconds
Triceps Push-Ups	30 seconds
Jumping Jack Variations	25 seconds
Curl-Up Challenges	30 seconds
Gallop	25 seconds
Push-Up Challenges	30 seconds
Aerobic Bouncing and Clapping	25 seconds
Leg Extensions	30 seconds
Walking to cool down	25 seconds

Select music which has a strong rhythm and easy-to-hear beat. When the music is on students perform aerobic activities (for 25 seconds). When the music is not playing, students perform the strength development and flexibility exercises (30 seconds).

See text, p. 174-186 for descriptions of exercises. See text, p. 163-167 for descriptions of challenges.

Use scatter formation.

Lesson Focus -- Fundamental Skills through Relays

Relays

Beanbag Pass Relay

Players are in a line, standing side by side. The player on the right starts the beanbag, which is passed from one player to the next down the line. When it gets to the end of the line, the relay is over. The teacher should be sure that each player handles the bag. Children should rotate positions in line.

Circle Beanbag Pass Relay

Players stand in a circle, facing out, but close enough so that the beanbag can be handed from player to player. One circuit begins and ends with the same player. The underleg pass can be used in this formation also.

Carry-and-Fetch Relay

Players are in closed squad formation, with a hoop or circle positioned up to 30 feet in front of each team. The first runner on each team has a beanbag. On the command "Go," this player carries the beanbag forward and puts it inside the hoop, then returns and tags off the next runner. The second runner goes forward, picks up the beanbag, and hands it off to the third runner. One runner carries the beanbag forward and the next runner fetches it back. Different locomotor movements can be specified.

Lane Relays without Equipment

In lane relays, each runner runs in turn. The race is over when the last runner finishes. Lane relays are usually regular relays. Different types of movements can be used to challenge the runners.
    a. Locomotor movements: Walking, running, skipping, hopping, galloping, sliding, jumping

Relays teach cooperative skills because all students must follow specific rules to reach common goals. Relays are **not** useful for teaching motor skills as they focus on competition rather than proper skill performance. All relays in this chapter require a low level of skill, i.e., running, jumping, and so on. Because these skills have been overlearned by this age students, relays in this chapter can be completed successfully by all students.

Placing less skilled players in the first or last position of the relay team will force these students to perform in front of the class and reveal to others that they are inferior. To avoid this situation, place less skilled students in the middle of the team. Discretion can be used when moving players to avoid labeling them as unskilled performers.

b Stunt and animal movements such as the Puppy Dog Run, Seal Crawl, Bear Walk, Rabbit Jump, Frog Jump, and Crab Walk.

Partner Relays without Equipment

a. Children run (walk, skip, gallop, hop) with partners (inside hands joined) just as a single runner would.

b. Children face each other with hands joined (as partners), slide one way to a turning point, and slide back to the starting point---leading with the other side.

Rescue Relay

Lane formation is used, with the first runner behind a line about 30 feet in front of the team. The first runner runs back to the team, takes the first player in line by the hand, and "rescues" him by leading him back to the 30-foot line. The player who has just been rescued then runs back to the team and gets the next player, and so on, until the last player has been conducted to the line.

Attention Relay

The players on each team are facing forward in lane formation with team members about arms' distance apart. The distance between the teams should be about 10 feet. Two turning points are established for each team---one 10 feet in front of the team and the other 10 feet behind. Players are numbered consecutively from front to rear. The teacher calls, "Attention." All come to the attention position. The teacher calls out a number. The player on each team holding that number steps to the right, runs around the front and the back markers, and returns to place. The rest of the team runs in place. The first team to have all members at attention, including the returned runner, wins a point.

The numbers should not be called in consecutive order, but all numbers should be called. There must be enough distance between teams so that runners do not collide.

Skills that children have already learned should be used as the basis for movement in a relay. This implies restricting relays to types that emphasize learned locomotor skills. Teachers mistakenly think that practicing a skill in a relay is an effective way to learn. The truth of the matter is that youngsters concentrate on the outcome of the relay rather than correctly performing the skill.

Teams should be restricted to four or five players. Too many on a team increases the amount of time spent waiting for a turn.

If teams have uneven numbers, some players on the smaller teams can run twice. All children on teams with fewer members must take a turn running twice; otherwise, the more skilled runners may always run and create an unfair advantage.

Teams should be changed regularly so that all youngsters have a chance to be on a winning team. Teachers should reserve the right to change team makeup as well as the order in which the students are placed on individual teams.

Game Activity

Wolfe's Beanbag Exchange

Supplies: One beanbag per child

Skills: Running, dodging, tossing, catching

Five or six children are identified as taggers. The remaining children start scattered throughout the area, each with a beanbag in hand. The taggers chase the players with beanbags. When a tag is made, the tagged player must freeze, keeping her feet still and beanbag in hand. To unfreeze a player, a non-frozen player can exchange his beanbag for a beanbag held by a frozen player. If two frozen players are within tossing distance, they can thaw each other by exchanging their beanbags through the air using a toss and catch. **Both** tosses have to be caught or the beanbags must be retrieved and tried again.

Variation: After students have learned the game, tell the taggers that they may interfere with the tossing of beanbags between two frozen players by batting them to the floor. This forces the toss to be tried again and the players remain frozen until successful catches are made by both players.

Arches

Supplies: Music

Skills: Moving rhythmically

The game is similar to London Bridge. An arch is placed in the playing area. (To form an arch, two players stand facing one another with hands joined and arms raised.) When the music starts, the other players move in a circle, passing under the arch. Suddenly, the music stops, and the arch is brought down by dropping the hands. All players caught in an arch immediately pair off to form other arches, keeping in a general circle formation. If a caught player does not have a partner, he waits in the center of the circle until one is available. The last players caught (or left) form arches for the next game.

The arches should be warned not to bring down their hands and arms too forcefully so that children passing under are not pummeled.

Variation: Different types of music can be used, and children can move according to the pattern of the music.

Lesson Plans for Grades 3-4 - Week 30
Rhythmic Movement with Equipment

Objectives:
To evade or stay near a partner while traveling
To perform rhythmic activities while handling manipulative equipment

Equipment Required:
Exercise to Music Tape
Two Lummi sticks for each student
One jump rope for each student
One playground ball for each student

Instructional Activities	Teaching Hints

Introductory Activity – Marking

Each child has a partner who is somewhat equal in ability. Under control, one partner runs, dodges, and tries to lose the other, who tries to stay within 3 ft of the runner. On signal, both freeze. The chaser must be close enough to touch her partner to say that they have marked (scored a point) them. Partners then reverse roles.

1. Use different locomotor movements.
2. Allow a point to be scored only when they touch a specified body part (i.e., knee, elbow, left hand).

Fitness Development Activity -- Exercises to Music

Side Flex (switch sides)	30 seconds	
Jogging	25 seconds	
Abdominal Challenges	30 seconds	
Slide or Skip	25 seconds	
Triceps Push-Ups	30 seconds	
Jumping Jack variations	25 seconds	
Curl-Up Challenges	30 seconds	
Gallop	25 seconds	
Push-Up challenges	30 seconds	
Aerobic Bouncing and Clapping	25 seconds	
Leg Extensions	30 seconds	
Walking to cool down	25 seconds	

Select music which has a strong rhythm and easy-to-hear beat. When the music is on students perform aerobic activities (for 25 seconds). When the music is not playing, students perform the strength development and flexibility exercises (30 seconds).

See text, p. 174-186 for descriptions of exercises. See text, p. 163-167 for descriptions of challenges.

Use scatter formation.

Lesson Focus -- Rhythmic Movement with Equipment

Rope Jumping Skills to Music
1. Perform the slow-time and fast-time rhythm with the rope held in one hand and turned.
2. Jump the rope and practice changing back and forth from slow to fast time.
3. Review basic steps student have learned in the earlier lesson plan on rope jumping (lesson plan #14).
4. Allow student time to put together a simple routine to music using some of the steps they have learned.

Ball Skills to Music
Perform a number of ball skills to the rhythm of the music. See lesson plan #8 for a refresher of skills learned previously.
    a. Bounce and catch.
    b. Bounce, clap, catch; bounce, turn, catch--also use toss.
    c. Dribble continuously in place and while moving.
    d. Work with a partner or in groups, passing one or more balls to one another in rhythm.
    e. Develop a routine utilizing some of the skills above.

Music selected should have a steady and unchanging beat. It should be played loud so that it can easily be heard above the noise of jump ropes and/or balls.

Jumping rope is a demanding activity. Even though music will motivate youngsters to practice, it can't be done for long. Take a break and practice ball skills. If desired, come back to rope jumping after practicing ball skills.

Encourage students to bounce the ball on the beat of the rhythm. It may help to hit a tom-tom or tambourine to make the beat easy to feel.

Lummi Sticks

Records: KIM 2000, 2014, 2015; HLP Lummi Sticks
Formation: Couples scattered throughout the area
Directions: Lummi sticks are smaller versions of wands; they are 12 to 15 inches long. Most Lummi stick activities are done by partners, although some can be done individually. Each child sits cross-legged, facing a partner at a distance of 18 to 20 inches. Children adjust this distance as the activities demand. The sticks are held in the thumb and fingers (not the fist) at about the bottom third of the stick. Routines are based on sets of six movements; each movement is completed in one count. The following one-count movements are used to make up routines.

a. Vertical tap: Tap both sticks upright on the floor.

b. Partner tap: Tap partner's stick (right stick to right stick, or left to left).

c. End tap: Tilt the sticks forward or sideward and tap the ends on the floor.

d. Cross-tap: Cross hands and tap the upper ends to the floor.

e. Side tap: Tap the upper ends to the side.

f. Flip: Toss the stick in air, giving it a half turn, and catch other end.

g. Tap together: Hold the sticks parallel and tap them together.

h. Toss right (or left): Toss the right-hand stick to partner's right hand, at the same time receiving partner's right-hand stick.

i. Pass: Lay the stick on the floor and pick up partner's stick.

j. Toss right and left: Toss quickly right to right and left to left, all in the time of one count.

A number of routines, incorporating the movements described, are presented here in sequence of difficulty. Each routine is to be done four times to complete the 24 beats of the chant.

a. Vertical tap, tap together, partner tap right, vertical tap, tap together, partner tap left.

b. Vertical tap, tap together, pass right stick, vertical tap, tap together, pass left stick.

c. Vertical tap, tap together, toss right stick, vertical tap, tap together, toss left stick.

d. Repeat numbers 1, 2, and 3, but substitute an end tap and flip for the vertical tap and tap together. Perform the stated third movement (e.g., end tap, flip, partner tap right, end tap, flip, partner tap left).

e. Vertical tap, tap together, toss right and left quickly, end tap, flip, toss right and left quickly.

f. Cross-tap, cross-flip, vertical tap (uncross arms), cross-tap, cross-flip, vertical tap (uncross arms).

Game Activity

Alaska Baseball

Supplies: A volleyball or soccer ball

Skills: Kicking, batting, running, ball handling

The players are organized in two teams, one of which is at bat while the other is in the field. A straight line provides the only out-of-bounds line, and the team at bat is behind this line at about the middle. The other team is scattered around the fair territory.

One player propels the ball, either batting a volleyball or kicking a stationary soccer ball. His teammates are in a close file behind him. As soon as the batter sends the ball into the playing area, he starts to run around his own team. Each time the runner passes the head of the file, the team gives a loud count.

There are no outs. The first fielder to get the ball stands still and starts to pass the ball back overhead to the nearest teammate, who moves directly behind to receive it. The remainder of the team in the field must run to the ball and form a file behind it. The ball is passed back overhead, with each player handling the ball. When the last field player in line has a firm grip on it, she shouts "Stop." At this signal, a count is made of the number of times the batter ran around his own team. To score more sharply, half rounds should be counted.

Five batters or half of the team should bat; then the teams should change places. This is better than allowing an entire team to bat before changing to the field, because players in the field tire from many consecutive runs.

Variation: Regular bases can be set up, and the batter can run the bases. Scoring can be in terms of a home run made or not; or the batter can continue around the bases, getting a point for each base.

Addition Tag

Supplies: None

Skills: Running, dodging

Two couples are it, and each stands with inside hands joined. These are the taggers. The other children run individually. The couples move around the playground, trying to tag with the free hands. The first person tagged joins the couple, making a trio. The three then chase until they catch a fourth. Once a fourth person is caught, the four divide and form two couples, adding another set of taggers to the game. This continues until all children are tagged.

Teaching suggestions: Some limitation of area should be established to enable the couples to catch the runners; otherwise, the game moves slowly and is fatiguing. The game moves faster if started with two couples. A tag is legal only when the couple or group of three keeps their hands joined. The game can be used as an introductory activity, since all children are active.

Lesson Plans for Grades 3-4 - Week 31
Track and Field-Related Activities (1)

Objectives:
To understand how to stretch prior to strenuous activity
To recognize the wide range of individual differences among peers

Equipment Required:
Stopwatches
Track and field equipment

Instructional Activities	Teaching Hints

Introductory and Fitness Development Activities – Stretching and Jogging

Combine the introductory and fitness activities during the track and field unit. This will help students understand how to stretch and warm up for demanding activity such as track and field.

Jog	1-2 minutes
Standing Hip Bend	30 seconds
Sitting Stretch	30 seconds
Partner Rowing	60 seconds
Bear Hug (stretch each leg)	40 seconds
Side Flex (stretch each leg)	40 seconds
Trunk Twister	30 seconds
Jog	3-4 minutes

Emphasis should be on jogging and stretching to prepare for strenuous activity.

Encourage smooth and controlled stretching. Hold each stretch for 6 to 10 seconds.

See text, p. 174-186 for descriptions of exercises.

Lesson Focus -- Track and Field-Related Activities (1)

Skills

Standing Start

The standing start should be practiced, for this type of start has a variety of uses in physical education activities. Many children find it more comfortable than the sprinter's start. When practical, however, children should use the sprinter's start for track work. In the standing start, the feet should be in a comfortable half-stride position. An extremely long stride is to be avoided. The body leans forward so that the center of gravity is forward. The weight is on the toes, and the knees are flexed slightly. The arms can be down or hanging slightly back.

Sprinter's Start

There are several kinds of sprinter's starts, but teachers are advised to concentrate on a single one. The "On your mark" position places the toe of the front foot from 4 to 12 inches behind the starting line. The thumb and first finger are just behind the line, with other fingers adding support. The knee of the rear leg is placed just opposite the front foot or ankle.

For the "Get set" position, the seat is raised so that it is nearly parallel to the ground. The knee of the rear leg is raised off the ground, and the shoulders are moved forward over the hands. The weight is evenly distributed over the hands and feet. The head is not raised, as the runner should be looking at a spot a few feet in front of the starting line.

On the "Go" signal, the runner pushes off sharply with both feet, with the front leg straightening as the back leg comes forward for a step. The body should rise gradually rather than pop up suddenly. The instructor should watch for a stumbling action on the first few steps. This results from too much weight resting on the hands in the "Get set" position.

Sprinting

In proper sprinting form, the body leans forward, with the arms swinging in opposition to the legs. The arms are bent at the elbows and swing from the shoulders in a forward and backward plane, not across the body. Forceful arm action aids sprinting. The knees are lifted sharply forward and upward and are brought down with a vigorous motion, followed by a forceful push from the toes.

The goal of track and field is self-improvement and developing proper techniques. Each student must accept responsibility for self-directed work and should be encouraged to try all activities.

The program should offer something for all---boys and girls, the highly skilled and the less skilled, and those with physical problems. Children with weight problems need particular attention. They must be stimulated and encouraged, since their participation will be minimal if little attention is paid to them. Special goals can be set for overweight children, and special events and goals can also be established for children with handicaps.

The long jump must be maintained properly. It should be filled with fresh sand of a coarse variety.

Distance Running

In distance running, as compared with sprinting, the body is more erect and the motion of the arms is less pronounced. Pace is an important consideration. Runners should try to concentrate on the qualities of lightness, ease, relaxation, and looseness. Good striding action, a slight body lean, and good head position are also important. Runners should be encouraged to strike the ground with the heel first and then push off with the toes.

Standing Long Jump

In the standing long jump, the jumper toes the line with feet flat on the ground and fairly close together. The arms are brought forward in a preliminary swing and are then swung down and back. The jump is made with both feet as the arms are swung forcibly forward to assist in lifting the body upward and forward. In the air, the knees should be brought upward and forward, with the arms held forward to sustain balance.

Long Jump

For the running long jump, a short run is needed. The run should be timed so that the toes of the jumping foot contact the board in a natural stride. The jumper takes off from one foot and strives for height. The landing is made on both feet after the knees have been brought forward. The landing should be in a forward direction, not sideward.

A fair jump takes off behind the scratch line. A foul (scratch) jump is called if the jumper steps beyond the scratch line or runs into or through the pit. Each contestant is given a certain number of trials (jumps). A scratch jump counts as a trial. Measurement is from the scratch line to the nearest point of touch.

Drills - Station (Small Group) Instruction

Divide the group into four groups and send an equal number of students to each station. Practice the skills at each station. Finish the lesson by running the relay activities listed in the game section below.

Station 1 - Starting and Sprinting

Practice starting form. Work with a partner who gives the commands for starting. Sprint 40 to 60 yards and walk back to the starting line. Reverse roles.

Station 2 - Standing Long Jump

The standing long jump can be done on a tumbling mat or the ground. A tape measure can be taped to the mat or placed on the ground so students can see how far they are jumping. Swing the arms forward on the takeoff.

Station 3 - Running Long Jump

Practice the running long jump by taking a short run, making contact with the takeoff board and jumping into the pit.

Station 4 - Distance Running for Pace

Outline a track with cones and have children run at a pace they can continue. If they need to stop frequently, they are running too fast. The running should be loose and relaxed. Work at this station is for learning a proper pace rather than racing.

The goal of the program should be to allow students to develop at their own rate. The instructor needs to be perceptive enough to determine whether students are working too hard or too little. Special attention must be given to those who appear disinterested, dejected, emotionally upset, or withdrawn.

If stop watches and tape measures are used, it is important to make them highly visible. Tie bright colored cord to them or anchor to cones to assure that they are not misplaced.

Make signs for each of the stations. The signs should include appropriate performance techniques, what is to be done at each station, and appropriate safety precautions.

Game Activity

Potato Shuttle Relay

A small box about a foot square is placed 5 ft in front of each lane. Four 12-in. circles are drawn at 5-ft intervals beyond the box. This makes the last circle 25 ft from the starting point. Four blocks or beanbags are needed for each team.

To start, the blocks are placed in the box in front of each team. The first runner goes to the box, takes a single block, and puts it into one of the circles. She repeats this performance until there is a block in each circle; then she tags off the second runner. This runner brings the blocks back to the box, one at a time, and tags off the third runner, who returns the blocks to the circles, and so on.

Using a box to receive the blocks makes a definite target. When the blocks are taken to the circles, some rules must be made regarding placement. The blocks should be considered placed only when they are inside or touching a line. Blocks outside need to be replaced before the runner can continue. Paper plates or frisbees can be used instead of circles drawn on the floor.

Variation: The race can also be done with bowling pins. Instead of being placed in a box, they are in a large circle at the start.

Shuttle Relays

Since children are running toward each other, one great difficulty in running shuttle relays is control of the exchange. In the excitement, the next runner may leave too early, and the tag or exchange is then made ahead of the restraining line. A high-jump standard or cone can be used to prevent early exchanges. The next runner awaits the tag with an arm around the standard or a hand on a cone.

One on One Contests

Allow students to find a friend and have a number of personal contests in track and field events such as sprints, hurdling, high jump, and standing long jump.

Lesson Plans for Grades 3-4 - Week 32
Track and Field-Related Activities (2)

Objectives:
To understand how to stretch prior to strenuous activity
To recognize the wide range of individual differences among peers

Equipment Required:
Stopwatches
Track and Field Equipment

Instructional Activities	Teaching Hints

Introductory and Fitness Development Activities -- Stretching and Jogging

Combine the introductory and fitness activities during the track and field unit. This will help students understand how to stretch and warm up for demanding activity such as track and field.

Jog	1-2 minutes	
Standing Hip Bend	30 seconds	
Sitting Stretch	30 seconds	
Partner Rowing	60 seconds	
Bear Hug (stretch each leg)	40 seconds	
Side Flex (stretch each leg)	40 seconds	
Trunk Twister	30 seconds	
Jog	3-4 minutes	

Emphasis should be on jogging and stretching to prepare for strenuous activity.

Encourage smooth and controlled stretching. Hold each stretch for 6 to 10 seconds

See text, p. 174-186 for descriptions of exercises

Lesson Focus -- Track and Field-Related Activities

Skills
Review the skills taught in the previous lesson. Introduce the following skills:
Baton Passing

The right hand to left hand method is used in longer distance relays and is the best choice for elementary school children as it is easy and offers a consistent method for passes. This pass allows the receiver to face the inside of the track while waiting to receive the baton in the left hand. The oncoming runner holds the baton in the right hand like a candle when passing it to a teammate. The receiver reaches back with the left hand, fingers pointing down and thumb to the inside, and begins to run as the runner advances to within 3 to 5 yards. The receiver grasps the baton and shifts it from the left to the right hand while moving. If the baton is dropped, it must be picked up, or the team is disqualified. An alternative way to receive the baton is to reach back with the hand facing up; however, the fingers-down method is considered more suitable for sprint relays.

Hop-Step-and-Jump

The hop-step-and-jump event requires a takeoff board and a jumping pit. The distance from the takeoff board to the pit should be one that even less skilled jumpers can make. The event begins with a run similar to that for the running long jump. The takeoff is with one foot, and the jumper must land on the same foot to complete the hop. He then takes a step followed by a jump. The event finishes like the long jump, with a landing on both feet. The pattern can be changed to begin with the left foot.

The jumper must not step over the takeoff board in the first hop, under penalty of fouling. Distance is measured from the front of the takeoff board to the closest place where the body touches. This is usually a mark made by one of the heels, but it could be a mark made by an arm or another part of the body if the jumper landed poorly and fell backward.

Drills - Station (Small Group) Instruction
Divide the group into four groups and send an equal number of students to each station. Practice the skills at each station. Finish the lesson by running the relay activities listed in the game section below.

The goal of track and field is self-improvement and developing proper techniques. Each student must accept responsibility for self-directed work and should be encouraged to try all activities.

The program should offer something for all---boys and girls, the highly skilled and the less skilled, and those with physical problems. Children with weight problems need particular attention. They must be stimulated and encouraged, since their participation will be minimal if little attention is paid to them. Special goals can be set for overweight children, and special events and goals can also be established for children with handicaps.

Pits for the long jump and the hop-step-and-jump must be maintained properly. They should be filled with fresh sand of a coarse variety.

The goal of the program should be to allow students to develop at their own rate. The instructor needs to be perceptive enough to determine whether students are working too hard or too little. Special attention must be given to those who appear disinterested, dejected, emotionally upset, or withdrawn.

Station 1 - Starting and Sprinting

Practice starting form. Work with a partner who gives the commands for starting. Sprint 40 to 60 yards and walk back to the starting line. Reverse roles.

Station 2 - Hop-Step-and-Jump

Set up the hop-step-and-jump with instructions on proper form set on a cone.

Station 3 - Baton Passing

Practice the running long jump by taking a short run, making contact with the takeoff board and jumping into the pit.

Station 4 - Distance Running for Pace

Outline a track with cones and have children run at a pace they can continue. If they need to stop frequently, they are running too fast. The running should be loose and relaxed. Work at this station is for learning a proper pace rather than racing.

If stop watches and tape measures are used, it is important to make them highly visible. Tie bright colored cord to them or anchor to cones to assure that they are not misplaced.

Make signs for each of the stations. The signs should include appropriate performance techniques, what is to be done at each station, and appropriate safety precautions.

Game Activity

Circular (Pursuit) Relays

Circular relays make use of the regular circular track. The baton exchange technique is important, and practice is needed. On a 220-yard or 200-meter track, relays can be organized in a number of ways, depending on how many runners are spaced for one lap. Four runners can do a lap, each running one quarter of the way; two can do a lap, each running one half of the distance; or each runner can complete a whole lap. In these races, each member of the relay team runs the same distance. Relays can also be organized so that members run different distances.

Shuttle Relays

Since children are running toward each other, one great difficulty in running shuttle relays is control of the exchange. In the excitement, the next runner may leave too early, and the tag or exchange is then made ahead of the restraining line. A high-jump standard or cone can be used to prevent early exchanges. The next runner awaits the tag with an arm around the standard or a hand on a cone.

One on One Contests

Allow students to find a friend and have a number of personal contests in track and field events such as sprints, hurdling, high jump, and standing long jump.

Lesson Plans for Grades 3-4 - Week 33
Fundamental Skills Using Parachute Activities

Objectives:
To design a personalized warm-up routine
To work together with peers to accomplish parachute activities
To develop strength through parachute activities

Equipment Required:
Signs for Hexagon Hustle
Parachute
Box and 4 balls

Instructional Activities		Teaching Hints

Introductory Activity -- Creative Routine

Each student should develop his own warm-up routine. Youngsters should be encouraged to use a combination of locomotor activities and stretching activities.

Offer direction if a student has difficulty creating their personal warm-up.

Fitness Development Activity -- Hexagon Hustle

Hustle	20 seconds	Outline a large hexagon with six cones.
Push-Up from Knees	30 seconds	Place signs with directions on both sides
Hustle	20 seconds	of the cones. The signs identify the hustle
Bend and Twist (8 counts)	30 seconds	activity students are to perform as they
Hustle	20 seconds	approach a cone. Tape alternating
Jumping Jacks (4 counts)	30 seconds	segments of silence and music to signal
Hustle	20 seconds	duration of exercise. Music segments
Abdominal Challenges (2 counts)	30 seconds	indicate aerobic activity while intervals
Hustle	20 seconds	of silence announce flexibility and
Double Leg Crab Kick	30 seconds	strength development activities.
Hustle	20 seconds	
Sit and Stretch (8 counts)	30 seconds	See text, p. 174-186 for descriptions of
Hustle	20 seconds	exercises.
Power Jumper	30 seconds	
Hustle	20 seconds	See text, p. 194 for description of
Squat Thrust (4 counts)	30 seconds	Hexagon Hustle.

Lesson Focus -- Parachute Activities

Parachute Warm-Up Activities. These activities are useful for starting children on the parachute. They are demanding activities which allow students to use excess energy.

Shaking the Rug and Making Waves

Shaking the Rug involves rapid movements of the parachute, either light or heavy. Making Waves involves large movements to send billows of cloth up and down.

Chute Crawl

Half of the class, either standing or kneeling, stretches the chute at waist level parallel to the ground. The remaining children crawl under the chute to the opposite side from their starting position.

Kite Run

The class holds the chute on one side with one hand. The leader points in the direction they are to run while holding the chute aloft like a kite.

Running Number Game

The children around the chute count off by fours; then they run lightly, holding the chute in one hand. The teacher calls out one of the numbers. Children with that number immediately release their grip on the chute and run forward to the next place vacated. They must put on a burst of speed to move ahead.

Parachute Exercise Activities. Exercises should be done vigorously and with enough repetitions to challenge the children. In addition to the exercises presented, others can be adapted to parachute play.

One parachute is generally sufficient for a class of 30 children. Parachutes come in different sizes, but those with diameters ranging from 24 to 32 feet are suitable for a regular class. The size with most utility is the 28-foot parachute. Each parachute has an opening near the top to allow trapped air to escape and to keep the parachute shaped properly. Most parachutes are constructed of nylon. A parachute should stretch tight and not sag in the middle when it is pulled on by children spaced around it.

The grips used in handling the parachute are comparable to those employed in hanging activities on an apparatus. Grips can be with one or two hands, overhand (palms facing away), underhand (palms facing toward), or mixed (one hand underhand and the other overhand).

Toe Toucher

Sit with feet extended under the parachute and hold the chute taut with a two-hand grip, drawing it up to the chin. Bend forward and touch the grip to the toes. Return parachute to stretched position.

Curl-Up

Extend the body under the parachute in curl-up position, so that the chute comes up to the chin when held taut. Do Curl-Ups, returning each time to the stretched chute position.

Dorsal Lift

Lie prone, with head toward the parachute and feet pointed back, away from it. Grip the chute and slide toward the feet until there is some tension on it. Raise the chute off the ground with a vigorous lift of the arms, until head and chest rise off the ground. Return.

V-Sit

Lie supine, with head toward the chute. Do V-Ups by raising the upper and lower parts of the body simultaneously into a V-shaped position. The knees should be kept straight.

Backward Pull

Face the parachute and pull back, away from its center. Pulls can be made from a sitting, kneeling, or standing position.

Parachute Activities with Equipment These are excellent activities for teaching youngsters to work together.

Ball Circle

Place a basketball or a cageball on the raised chute. Make the ball roll around the chute in a large circle, controlling it by raising or lowering the chute. Try the same with two balls. A beach ball is also excellent.

Popcorn

Place a number of beanbags (from six to ten) on the chute. Shake the chute to make them rise like corn popping.

Team Ball

Divide the class in half, each team defending half of the chute. Using from two to six balls of any variety, try to bounce the balls off the opponents' side, scoring 1 point for each ball.

Poison Snake

Divide into teams. Place from 6 to 10 jump ropes on the chute. Shake the chute and try to make the ropes hit players on the other side. For each rope that touches one team member, that team has a point scored against it. The team with the lower score is the winner.

Parachute Dome Activities Dome activities are favorites of youngsters. They demand that all youngsters work together to lift the chute and place it on the floor. To make a dome, children begin with the parachute on the floor, holding with two hands and kneeling on one knee. To trap air under the chute, children stand up quickly, thrusting their arms above the head, and then return to starting position.

Students under the Chute

Tasks for under the chute can be specified, such as turning a certain number of turns with a jump rope, throwing and catching a beanbag, or bouncing a ball a number of times. The needed objects should be under the chute before the dome is made.

Number Exchange

Children are numbered from one to four. The teacher calls a number as the dome is made, and those with the number called must change position to be under the dome before the chute comes down. Locomotor movements can be varied.

Punching Bag

Children make a dome and stand on the edges. They then punch at the chute while slowly and gently walking the edges of the chute toward the center.

For preliminary explanations, the parachute can be stretched out on the ground in its circular pattern, with the children seated so that they cannot touch the parachute during instructions. When the children hold the parachute during later explanations, they should retain their hold lightly, letting the center of the parachute drop to the ground. Children must be taught to exercise control and not to manipulate the parachute while explanations are in progress.

Walking on the parachute should be discouraged, since it is a slippery surface and may increase the chance of falls.

Teach the proper technique of lifting the parachute. Youngsters should start with one knee on the floor; as the hands lift upward, stand and make the legs do the work. As the stand occurs, take a step toward the center of the chute and lift upward. Lifting should be done with the legs and arms.

Blooming Flower

Children make a dome and kneel with both knees on the edge of the chute. Youngsters hold hands around the chute and lean in and out to represent a blooming flower opening.

Lights Out

While making a dome, the children take two steps toward the center and sit inside the chute. The chute can be held with the hands at the side or by sitting on it.

Mushroom Activities

To form a mushroom, students begin with the chute on the ground, kneeling on one knee and holding with two hands. They stand up quickly, thrusting the arms overhead. Keeping the arms overhead, each walks forward three or four steps toward the center. The arms are held overhead until the chute is deflated.

Mushroom Release

All children release at the peak of inflation and either run out from under the chute or move to the center and sit down, with the chute descending on top of them.

Mushroom Run

Children make a mushroom. As soon as they move into the center, they release holds and run once around the inside of the chute, counterclockwise, back to place.

Game Activity

Nonda's Car Lot

Supplies: None

Skills: Running, dodging

One player is it and stands in the center of the area between two lines established about 50 ft apart. The class selects four brands of cars (e.g., Honda, Corvette, Toyota, Cadillac). Each student then selects a car from the four but does not tell anyone what it is.

The tagger calls out a car name. All students who selected that name attempt to run to the other line without getting tagged. The tagger calls out the cars until all students have run. When a child (car) gets tagged, she must sit down at the spot of the tag. She cannot move but may tag other students who run too near her. When the one who is it calls out "Car lot," all of the cars must go. The game is played until all students have been tagged.

Box Ball

Supplies: A sturdy box, 2 ft square and about 12 in. deep; four volleyballs (or similar balls)

Skills: Running, ball handling

The class is divided into four even teams, with six to ten players per team. Each team occupies one side of a hollow square at an equal distance from the center. Players face inward and number off consecutively from right to left.

A box containing four balls is put in the center. The instructor calls a number, and the player from each team who has that number runs forward to the box, takes a ball, and runs to the head of his line, taking the place of player 1. In the meantime, the players in the line have moved to the left just enough to fill in the space left by the runner. On reaching the head of the line, the runner passes the ball to the next person and so on down the line to the end child. The last child runs forward and returns the ball to the box. The first team to return the ball to the box scores a point.

The runner must not pass the ball down the line until he is in place at the head of the line. The ball must be caught and passed by each child. Failure to conform to these rules results in team disqualification. Runners stay at the head of the line, retaining their original number. Keeping the lines in consecutive number sequence is not important.

Lesson Plans for Grades 3-4 - Week 34
Manipulative Skills Using Frisbees

Objectives:
To learn the unique throwing style required with frisbees
To learn the rules of frisbee golf
To perform continuous fitness activity

Equipment Required:
Cones
One Frisbee per student
Hoops and Bowling Pins
Signs for Hexagon Hustle

Instructional Activities	Teaching Hints

Introductory Activity -- Four-Corners Movement

Lay out a rectangle with a cone at each corner. As the child passes each corner, he changes to a different locomotor movement.

Challenge the students by declaring various qualities of movement (i.e., soft, heavy, slow, fast).

Fitness Development Activity -- Hexagon Hustle

Hustle	25 seconds	Outline a large hexagon with six cones.
Push-Up from Knees	30 seconds	Place signs with directions on both sides
Hustle	25 seconds	of the cones. The signs identify the hustle
Bend and Twist (8 counts)	30 seconds	activity students are to perform as they
Hustle	25 seconds	approach a cone. Tape alternating
Jumping Jacks (4 counts)	30 seconds	segments of silence and music to signal
Hustle	25 seconds	duration of exercise. Music segments
Abdominal Challenges (2 counts)	30 seconds	indicate aerobic activity while intervals
Hustle	25 seconds	of silence announce flexibility and
Double Leg Crab Kick	30 seconds	strength development activities.
Hustle	25 seconds	
Sit and Stretch (8 counts)	30 seconds	Encourage students to do their best.
Hustle	25 seconds	
Power Jumper	30 seconds	See text, p. 174-186 for descriptions of
Hustle	25 seconds	exercises. See text, p. 194 for
Squat Thrust (4 counts)	30 seconds	descriptions of Hexagon Hustle.

Lesson Focus -- Manipulative Skills Using Frisbees

Throwing the Disk

Backhand Throw

The backhand grip is used most often. The thumb is on top of the disk, the index finger along the rim, and the other fingers underneath. To throw the Frisbee with the right hand, stand in a sideways position with the right foot toward the target. Step toward the target and throw the Frisbee in a sideways motion across the body, snapping the wrist and trying to keep the disk flat on release.

Underhand Throw

The underhand throw uses the same grip as in the backhand throw, but the thrower faces the target and holds the disk at the side of the body. Step forward with the leg opposite the throwing arm while bringing the Frisbee forward. When the throwing arm is out in the front of the body, release the Frisbee. The trick to this throw is learning to release the disk so that it is parallel to the ground.

Catching the Disk

Thumb-Down Catch

The thumb-down catch is used for catching when the disk is received at waist level or above. The thumb is pointing toward the ground. The Frisbee should be tracked from the thrower's hand. This clues the catcher about any tilt on the disk that may cause it to curve.

Thumb-Up Catch

The thumb-up catch is used when the Frisbee is received below waist level. The thumb points up, and the fingers are spread.

Use the following instructional cues to improve skill performance:

a. Release the disk parallel to the ground. If it is tilted, a curved throw results.

b. Step toward the target and follow through on release of the disk.

c. Snap open the wrist and make the Frisbee spin.

If space is limited, all Frisbees should be thrown in the same direction. Students can line up on either side of the area and throw across to each other.

Most activities are best practiced by pairs of students using one disk.

Throwing and Catching Activities:

a. Throw the Frisbee at different levels to partner.
b. Throw a curve--to the left, right and upward. Vary the speed of the curve.
c. Throw a bounce pass--try a low and a high pass.
d. Throw the disc like a boomerang. Must throw at a steep angle into the wind.
e. Throw the Frisbee into the air, run and catch. Increase the distance of the throw.
f. Throw the Frisbee through a hoop held by a partner.
g. Catch the Frisbee under your leg. Catch it behind your back.
h. Throw the Frisbees into hoops that are placed on the ground as targets. Different-colored hoops can be given different values. Throw through your partner's legs.
i. Frisbee bowling--One partner has a bowling pin which the other partner attempts to knock down by throwing the Frisbee.
j. Play catch while moving. Lead your partner so he doesn't have to break stride.
k. See how many successful throws and catches you can make in 30 seconds.
l. Frisbee Baseball Pitching--Attempt to throw the Frisbee into your partner's "Strike Zone."

Youngsters can develop both sides of the body by learning to throw and catch the disk with either hand. The teacher should design the activities so that youngsters get both right-hand and left-hand practice.

Since a Frisbee is somewhat different from the other implements that children usually throw, devote some time to teaching form and style in throwing and catching. Avoid drills that reward speed in throwing and catching.

Game Activity

Frisbee Keep Away

Supplies: Frisbees
Skills: Throwing and catching Frisbees

Students break into groups of three. Two of the players in the group try to keep the other player from touching the Frisbee while they are passing it back and forth. If the Frisbee is touched by the defensive player, the person who through the Frisbee becomes the defensive player. Begin the game by asking students to remain stationary while throwing and catching. Later, challenge can be added by allowing all players in the group move.

Frisbee Golf

Supplies: One Frisbee per person, hoops for hole markers, cones
Skills: Frisbee throwing for accuracy

Frisbee Golf or disk golf is a favorite game of many students. Boundary cones with numbers can be used for tees, and holes can be boxes, hula hoops, trees, tires, garbage cans, or any other available equipment on the school grounds. Draw a course on a map for students and start them at different holes to decrease the time spent waiting to tee off. Regulation golf rules apply. The students can jog between throws for increased activity.

Disk golf is played like regular golf. One stroke is counted for each time the disk is thrown and when a penalty is incurred. The object is to acquire the lowest score. The following rules dictate play:

Tee-throws: Tee-throws must be completed within or behind the designated tee area.

Lie: The lie is the spot on or directly underneath the spot where the previous throw landed.

Throwing order: The player whose disk is the farthest from the hole throws first. The player with the least number of throws on the previous hole tees off first.

Fairway throws: Fairway throws must be made with the foot closest to the hole on the lie. A run-up is allowed.

Dog leg: A dog leg is one or more designated trees or poles in the fairway that must be passed on the outside when approaching the hole. There is a two-stroke penalty for missing a dog leg.

Putt throw: A putt throw is any throw within 10 ft of the hole. A player may not move past the point of the lie in making the putt throw. Falling or jumping putts are not allowed.

Unplayable lies: Any disk that comes to rest 6 ft or more above the ground is unplayable. The next throw must be played from a new lie directly underneath the unplayable lie (one-stroke penalty).

Out-of-bounds: A throw that lands out-of-bounds must be played from the point where the disk went out (one-stroke penalty).

Course courtesy: Do not throw until the players ahead are out of range.

Completion of hole: A disk that comes to rest in the hole (box or hoop) or strikes the designated hole (tree or pole) constitutes successful completion of that hole.

Lesson Plans for Grades 3-4 - Week 35
Softball Related Activities

Objectives:
To throw and catch a softball
To hit a softball
To be able to field softball grounders and fly balls

Equipment Required:
Softballs (or whiffle balls)
Bats (plastic bats for whiffle balls)
Batting tee and bases
Parachute and exercise music
Playground ball

Instructional Activities	Teaching Hints

Introductory Activity -- High Fives

Students move in different directions throughout the area. On signal, they are challenged to run toward a partner, jump, and give a "high five" (slap hands) while moving. Emphasis should be placed on timing so that the "high five" is given at the top of the jump.

Change the type of high fives, i.e., low, underleg, roundhouse.

High fives should be given gently. No hard slapping.

Fitness Development Activity -- Parachute Fitness

1. Jog in circle with chute held in left hand. Reverse directions and hold with right hand. (music)
2. Standing, raise the chute overhead, lower to waist, lower to toes, raise to waist, etc. (no music)
3. Slide to the right; return slide to the left. (music)
4. Sit and perform Abdominal Challenges. (no music)
5. Skip. (music)
6. Freeze; face the center, and stretch the chute tightly with bent arms. Hold for 8-12 seconds. Repeat five to six times. (no music)
7. Run in place, hold the chute at waist level and hit the chute with lifted knees. (music)
8. Sit with legs under the chute. Do a seat walk toward the center. Return to the perimeter. Repeat four to six times. (no music)
9. Place the chute on the ground. Jog away from the chute and return on signal. Repeat. (music)
10. On sides with legs under the chute, perform Side Flex and lift chute with legs. (no music)
11. Hop to the center of the chute and return. Repeat. (music)
12. Assume the push-up position with the legs aligned away from the center of the chute. Shake the chute with one arm while the other arm supports the body. (no music)
13. Lie on back with legs under the chute. Shake the chute with the feet. (music)
14. Sit with feet under the chute. Stretch by touching the toes with the chute. Relax with other stretches while sitting. (no music)

Tape alternating segments (25-30 seconds in length) of silence and music to signal duration of exercise. Music segments indicate aerobic activity with the parachute while intervals of silence announce using the chute to enhance flexibility and strength development.

Space youngsters evenly around the chute.

Use different hand grips (palms up, down, mixed).

All movements should be done under control. Some of the faster and stronger students will have to moderate their performance.

See text, p. 163-167 for descriptions of challenges.

Lesson Focus -- Softball-Related Activities

Skills
Practice the following skills:
1. Overhand Throw

In preparation for throwing, the child secures a firm grip on the ball, raises the throwing arm to shoulder height, and brings the elbow back. For the overhand throw, the hand with the ball is then brought back over the head so that it is well behind the shoulder at about shoulder height. The left side of the body is turned in the direction of the throw, and the left arm is raised in front of the body. The weight is on the back (right) foot, with the left foot advanced and the toe touching the ground. The arm comes forward with the elbow leading, and the ball is thrown with a downward snap of the wrist. The body weight is brought forward into the throw, shifting to the front foot. Follow-through so that the palm of the throwing hand faces the ground at completion of the throw. The eyes should be on the target throughout.

Whiffle balls and plastic bats are a much safer alternative for children this age. It is easier for them to swing plastic bats and the fear of getting hit by a softball will not be an issue.

Instructional cues for **throwing** are:
1. Place the throwing arm side of the body away from the target.
2. Step toward the target with the foot opposite the throwing hand.

3. Bend and raise the arm at the elbow. Lead with the elbow.

2. Pitching

Official rules call for the pitcher to have both feet in contact with the pitcher's rubber, but few elementary schools possess a rubber. Instead, the pitcher can stand with both feet about even, facing the batter, and holding the ball momentarily in front with both hands. The pitcher takes one hand from the ball, extends the right arm forward, and brings it back in a pendulum swing, positioning the ball well behind the body. A normal stride taken toward the batter with the left foot begins the throwing sequence for a right-handed pitcher. The arm is brought forward with an underhanded slingshot motion, and the weight is transferred to the leading foot. Only one step is permitted.

Instructional cues for **pitching** are:
1. Face the plate.
2. Keep your eyes on the target.
3. Swing the pitching arm backward and step forward.

3. Fielding Grounders

To field a grounder, the fielder should move as quickly as possible into the path of the ball and then move forward and play the ball on a good hop. The eyes must be kept on the ball, following it into the hands or glove. The feet are spread, the seat is kept down, and the hands are carried low and in front. The weight is on the balls of the feet or on the toes, and the knees are bent to lower the body. As the ball is caught, the fielder straightens up, takes a step in the direction of the throw, and makes the throw.

Instructional cues for **fielding** are:
1. Move into line with the path of the ball.
2. Give when catching the ball.
3. Use the glove to absorb the force of the ball.
4. For grounders, keep the head down and watch the ball move into the glove.

4. Batting (Right-Handed)

The batter stands with the left side of the body toward the pitcher. The feet are spread and the weight is on both feet. The body should be facing the plate. The bat is held with the trademark up, and the left hand grasps the bat lower than the right. The bat is held over the right shoulder, pointing both back and up. The elbows are away from the body. The swing begins with a hip roll and a short step forward in the direction of the pitcher. The bat is then swung level with the ground at the height of the pitch. The eyes are kept on the ball until it is hit. After the hit, there must be good follow-through.

Instructional cues for **batting** are:
1. Keep the hands together.
2. Swing the bat horizontally.
3. Swing through the ball.
4. Hold the bat off the shoulder.
5. Watch the ball hit the bat.

Station (Small Group) Instruction

Station 1 - Batting

Use a batting tee. For each station, two tees are needed, with a bat and at least two balls for each tee. Three to five children are assigned to each tee. There should be a batter, a catcher to handle incoming balls, and fielders. When only three children are in a unit, the catcher should be eliminated. Each batter is allowed a certain number of swings before rotating to the field. The catcher becomes the next batter, and a fielder moves up to catcher.

Hitters should avoid the following: lifting the front foot high off the ground, stepping back with the rear foot, or bending forward.

Station 2 - Throwing and Catching

Work with a partner and practice some of the following throwing drills:
    a. Throw back and forth, practicing various throws.
    b. gradually increase the distance of the throws.
    c. focus on accuracy; if the throws are not caught, reduce the distance between players

Stand about 7 to 10 yards apart when practicing throwing.

Station 3 - Pitching

Students find a partner and pitch and catch with each other. Set out a number of bases at each station so pitchers can pitch and catch using a base as a target (home plate).
    a. Pitch to another player over a plate.
    b. Call balls and strikes. One player is the pitcher, the second is the catcher, and the third is the umpire. A fourth player can be a stationary batter to provide a more realistic pitching target.

For youngsters who are afraid of the ball, use a whiffle ball.

Face the batter, both feet on the rubber and the ball held in front with both hands. One step is allowed, and the ball must be delivered on that step.
Ball must be pitched underhanded.
No motion or fake toward the plate can be made without delivering the ball.

Station 4 - Fielding

Players find a partner and practice throwing grounders and fly balls to each other.
    a. One partner throws a grounder, the other partner fields the ball and throws it back to the other. Reverse roles.
    b. Do the same thing above except throw fly balls.

Show form for high and low catch.

Move into the path of the ball.

Throw It and Run

Supplies: A softball or similar ball

Skills: Throwing, catching, fielding, base running

Throw-It-and-Run Softball is played like regular softball with the following exception. With one team in the field at regular positions, the pitcher throws the ball to the batter, who, instead of batting the ball, catches it and immediately throws it into the field. The ball is then treated as a batted ball, and regular softball rules prevail. No stealing is permitted, however, and runners must hold bases until the batter throws the ball. A foul ball is an out.

Variations:

1. Under-Leg Throw. Instead of throwing directly, the batter can turn to the right, lift the left leg, and throw the ball under the leg into the playing field.

2. Beat-Ball Throw. The fielders, instead of playing regular softball rules, throw the ball directly home to the catcher. The batter, in the meantime, runs around the bases. A point is scored for each base that she touches before the catcher receives the ball. A ball caught on the fly would mean no score. Similarly, a foul ball would not score points but would count as a turn at bat.

Two-Pitch Softball

Supplies: A softball, a bat

Skills: Most softball skills, except regular pitching

Two-Pitch Softball is played like regular softball with the following changes.

1. A member of the team at bat pitches. A system of rotation should be set up so that every child takes a turn as pitcher.

2. The batter has only two pitches in which to hit the ball, and he must hit a fair ball on one of these pitches or he is out. The batter can foul the first ball, but if he fouls the second, he is out. There is no need to call balls or strikes.

3. The pitcher does not field the ball. A member of the team in the field acts as the fielding pitcher.

4. If the batter hits the ball, regular softball rules are followed. No stealing is permitted, however.

Teaching suggestion: Since the pitcher is responsible for pitching a ball that can be hit, the pitching distance can be shortened to give the batter ample opportunity to hit the ball. The instructor can act as the pitcher.

Variation: <u>Three Strikes</u>: In this game, the batter is allowed three pitches (strikes) to hit the ball. Otherwise, the game proceeds as in Two-Pitch Softball.

Hit and Run

Supplies: A volleyball or soccer ball or playground ball, home plate, base markers

Skills: Catching, throwing, running, dodging

One team is at bat, and the other is scattered in the field. Boundaries must be established, but the area does not have to be shaped like a baseball diamond. The batter stands at home plate with the ball. In front of the batter, 12 ft away, is a short line over which the ball must be hit to be in play. In the center of the field, about 40 ft away, is the base marker.

The batter bats the ball with the hands or fists so that it crosses the short line and lands inside the area. She then attempts to run down the field, around the base marker, and back to home plate without being hit by the ball. The members of the other team field the ball and throw it at the runner. The fielder may not run or walk with the ball but may throw to a teammate who is closer to the runner.

A run is scored each time a batter runs around the marker and back to home plate without getting hit by the ball. A run also is scored if a foul is called on the fielding team for walking or running with the ball.

The batter is out in any of the following circumstances.

1. A fly ball is caught.

2. He is hit below the shoulders with the ball.

3. The ball is not hit beyond the short line.

4. The team touches home plate with the ball before the runner returns. (This out is used only when the runner stops in the field and does not continue.)

The game can be played in innings of three outs each, or a change of team positions can be made after all members of one team have batted.

Teaching suggestion: The distance the batter runs around the base marker may have to be shortened or lengthened, depending on player's ability.

Lesson Plans for Grades 3-4 - Week 36
Softball Related Activities

Objectives:
To throw and catch a softball
To hit a softball
To be able to field softball grounders and fly balls

Equipment Required:
Softballs (or whiffle balls)
Bats (plastic bats for whiffle balls)
Batting tee and bases
Parachute and exercise music
Soccer ball

Instructional Activities	Teaching Hints

Introductory Activity -- Small Group Movements

Organize class into small groups of 3-4 students. Each group moves around the area, following a leader. When a change is signaled, the last person goes to the head of the line and becomes the leader.

Encourage leaders to keep the group moving. The minimum activity is jogging in place.

Fitness Development Activity -- Parachute Fitness

1. Jog in circle with chute held in left hand. Reverse directions and hold with right hand. (music)
2. Standing, raise the chute overhead, lower to waist, lower to toes, raise to waist, etc. (no music)
3. Slide to the right; return slide to the left. (music)
4. Sit and perform Abdominal Challenges. (no music)
5. Skip. (music)
6. Freeze; face the center, and stretch the chute tightly with bent arms. Hold for 8-12 seconds. Repeat five to six times. (no music)
7. Run in place, hold the chute at waist level and hit the chute with lifted knees. (music)
8. Sit with legs under the chute. Do a seat walk toward the center. Return to the perimeter. Repeat four to six times. (no music)
9. Place the chute on the ground. Jog away from the chute and return on signal. Repeat. (music)
10. On sides with legs under the chute, perform Side Flex and lift chute with legs. (no music)
11. Hop to the center of the chute and return. Repeat. (music)
12. Assume the push-up position with the legs aligned away from the center of the chute. Shake the chute with one arm while the other arm supports the body. (no music)
13. Lie on back with legs under the chute. Shake the chute with the feet. (music)
14. Sit with feet under the chute. Stretch by touching the toes with the chute. Relax with other stretches while sitting. (no music)

Tape alternating segments (25-30 seconds in length) of silence and music to signal duration of exercise. Music segments indicate aerobic activity with the parachute while intervals of silence announce using the chute to enhance flexibility and strength development.

Space youngsters evenly around the chute.

Use different hand grips (palms up, down, mixed).

All movements should be done under control. Some of the faster and stronger students will have to moderate their performance.

See text, p. 163-167 for descriptions of challenges.

Lesson Focus -- Softball-Related Activities

Skills
Review skills learned last week:
1. Overhand Throw
2. Pitching
3. Fielding Grounders
4. Batting

Whiffle balls and plastic bats are a much safer alternative for children this age. It is easier for them to swing plastic bats and the fear of getting hit by a softball will not be an issue.

Station (Small Group) Instruction
Station 1 - Play Pepper (Hitting and Fielding)
A line of three or four players is about 10 yards in front of and facing a batter. The players toss the ball to the batter, who attempts to hit controlled grounders back to them. The batter stays at bat for a period of time and then rotates to the field.

If youngsters are not able to hit the ball, they can catch and throw it to the fielders.

Station 2 - Pitching and Umpiring

Students find a partner and pitch and catch with each other. Set out a number of bases at each station so pitchers can pitch and catch using a base as a target (home plate).

    a. Pitch to another player over a plate.

    b. Call balls and strikes. One player is the pitcher, the second is the catcher, and the third is the umpire. A fourth player can be a stationary batter to provide a more realistic pitching target.

When umpiring, strikes are called by raising the right hand and balls require raising the left hand.

Station 3 - Infield Practice

1. Throw around the bases clockwise and counterclockwise.
2. Roll ball to infielders and make the play at first. After each play, throw around the infield.
3. If enough skill, bat the ball to the infielders in turn.

While having infield practice, one person at the station can run the bases and try to complete a circuit around the bases before the ball does.

Station 4 - Batting Practice

Each batter takes six swings and then rotates to the field. Catcher becomes batter and pitcher moves up to catcher.

Have more than one ball at the stations so the pitching can continue when a ball is hit or not caught.

Game Activity

Kick Softball

    Supplies: A soccer ball or another ball to be kicked

    Skills: Kicking a rolling ball, throwing, catching, running bases

    The batter stands in the kicking area, a 3-ft-square home plate. The batter kicks the ball rolled on the ground by the pitcher. The ball should be rolled at moderate speed. An umpire calls balls and strikes. A strike is a ball that rolls over the 3-ft square. A ball rolls outside this area. Strikeouts and walks are called the same as in regular softball. The number of foul balls allowed should be limited. No base stealing is permitted. Otherwise, the game is played like softball.

Variations:

    1. The batter kicks a stationary ball. This saves time, since there is no pitching.

    2. Punch Ball. The batter can hit a volleyball as in a volleyball serve or punch a ball pitched by the pitcher.

In a Pickle

    Supplies: A softball, two bases 45 to 55 ft apart

    Skills: Throwing, catching, running down a base runner, tagging

    When a base runner gets caught between two bases and is in danger of being run down and tagged, she is "in a pickle." To begin, both fielders are on bases, one with a ball. The runner is positioned in the base path 10 to 15 ft away from the fielder with the ball. The two fielders throw the ball back and forth in an attempt to run down the runner between the bases and tag her. If the runner escapes and secures a base, she gets to try again. Otherwise, a system of rotation is established, including any sideline (waiting) players. No sliding is permitted.

Beat Ball

    Supplies: Soft softball, bat, batting tee (optional)

    Skills: All softball skills

    One team is at bat and the other team in the field. The object of the game is to hit the ball and run around the bases before the fielding team can catch the ball, throw it to first base, and then throw it to the catcher at home plate. If the ball beats the hitter home or a fly ball is caught, it is an out. If the hitter beats the ball to home plate, a run is scored. All players on a team bat once before switching positions with the fielding team. The ball must be hit into fair territory before the hitter can run. Only three pitches are allowed each hitter.

Variations:

    1. Depending on the maturity of the players, a batting tee may be used. The hitter can be allowed the option of using the batting tee or hitting a pitched ball.

    2. The pitcher can be selected from the batting team. This assures that an attempt will be made to make pitches that can be hit.

    3. The distance can be varied so that hitters have a fair opportunity to score. If hitters score too easily, another base can be added.